For E
with love

Bill Edelen

MW00892263

The Breath of Life

No tyranny can so bind human minds as religious tyranny. The reward for cutting through the chains is freedom........ freedom to pursue your spiritual quest with your very own insights and intuition. ......as you point your life....toward the source.....and toward the Mystery.

Self-Published by William L. Edelen

COPYRIGHT

The Breath of Life

Copyright © 2013 by William L. Edelen

All rights reserved. This includes the right to reproduce any portion of this book in any form.

Self-published with CreateSpace by William L. Edelen

First edition published in 2013

Other titles by the author: *Toward the Mystery; Spirit; Spirit Dance;* and *Earthrise*

Books > Religion > Essays >Spirituality > Humanism

Books > Native American > Mysticism

ISBN-13:
978-1484190166

ISBN-10:
1484190165

The Breath of Life

Essays by

William Edelen

"For Janet Gail whose love and light, with a shared vision, made this collection of essays possible. Her gift for my new "Breath of Life."

This book is a summation of the work and focus of my lifetime, up until this point of entering my 91st year. We have been inundated through television, radio and magazines with the evangelical, fundamentalist "born again" religious voice. My essays in this book have offered another option, to free the human mind from the cages, chains and mental concentration camps of the man made Christian dogmas and doctrines that have so killed and blocked the evolution of the human spirit. This book of essays is for those brave enough to examine the chains.

No tyranny can so bind human minds as religious tyranny. The reward for cutting through the chains is freedom...... freedom to pursue your spiritual quest with your very own insights and intuition. ......as you point your life....toward the source.....and toward the Mystery. That Mystery.....beyond human comprehension....doing we know not what....but whose presence saturates the universe....and wakens in us a sense of wonder and awe......participation in the Mystery of Being. I present this book of my essays to you for that purpose.

CONTENTS

CONTENTS continued

INTRODUCTION

The Lakota people have a beautiful and profound symbol for the "BREATH OF LIFE." Most American Indian traditions have a similar symbol for that vital "breath" that sustains our existence. It is Feathers. Feathers are the image of the invisible breath that fills our lungs with the energy to function as a human being.

A recent immediate crisis in my own life, with loss of breath, led me to the feathers. I had to respond without delay to the panic in my own life. I was breathless... literally. I reflected on the feathers available to me.

A first feather: The Western medical approach. Second feather: Eastern approach, with meditation, acupuncture, herbal. Third feather: Taoism and Zen... very comfortable for me.

I made the choice and selected the first feather, with many parts of the second and third feather as support for my condition.

Over the last 18 years the condition has been accumulating and came to a crisis where my breathing was impaired at my last Symposium on December 2nd. My local physician referred me to Dr. Ronald Himelman, a cardiologist.

After a trip to the Emergency Room at Desert Regional Medical Center, Dr. Himelman performed various tests and diagnosed Congestive Heart Failure due to a malfunctioning aortic valve. He followed up by contacting Dr. Raj Makkar at Cedars-Sinai Medical Center in Los Angeles to determine if I was a candidate for their ground-breaking interventional (catherization) valve replacement procedure they are performing there. This procedure is not available in most hospitals, including here in Palm Springs.

Realizing the critical urgency, a friend, Gail Brydges, to whom this book is dedicated, drove me for a full day of testing, including night time travel to Los Angeles and Cedars-Sinai Medical Center, and stayed with me throughout my days in the hospital.

The advice I received was that this was so critical the procedure needed to be immediate. It was a matter of life and death. An aortic valve is supposed to be the size of a quarter. Mine was the size of a pencil erasure...an opening near extinction with heavy calcification. It needed fixing immediately.

My mind unfolded to the Mayan calendar with which I am very familiar. December 21, 2012, is the date that the current cycle of the MAYAN ROUND CALENDAR ended...and the new era of the LONG CALENDAR began. It was, and is, a movement into a NEW CONSCIOUSNESS...A RENEWAL.

On Dec. 21....2012...I was told that I had a GIFT OF A NEW LIFE offered... a NEW HEART VALVE. So during that solstice week, on Christmas Eve to be exact, I underwent a TRANSCATHETER AORTIC VALVE REPLACEMENT (TAVR). It was literally for me a RENEWAL, and movement to a NEW CONSCIOUSNESS...a NEW BREATH OF LIFE and the inspiration for this NEW book of my essays and columns.

Dr. Raj Makkar of Cedars-Sinai Medical Center has been so successful with this minimally invasive surgery (not open heart surgery) that there will be a full wing for the tests and procedures of this technology when the new hospital facility opens in the summer of 2013.

As I lay in that hospital room, experiencing a very fast recovery...with normal breathing from the life giving oxygen filling my lungs...I thought what a precious gift is this Mystery called "Life"...a blessing in between two other mysteries, which are yet ONE. It is no wonder that to the Lakota, feathers became the symbol for the BREATH OF LIFE....and the inspiration for this new book of essays written by me, to honor this RENEWAL and NEW CONSCIOUSNESS given to me as set forth long ago by the Maya for December 2012.

REFLECTIONS AT AGE 90

On Tuesday, July 17th, 2012 I reached 90 years of age. As I reflect back on these years, it is fairly easy for me to find the thought, or thoughts, that have shaped my life, my outlook and attitudes, and guided my path regardless of criticism or attacks by those living in the boxes and cages they have chosen for their own confinement.

I realized that the key and path to MEDIOCRITY can be found in worry about the foolishness of public opinion, in "moderation"…in "convention" and "conformity". Two giant thinkers helped and encouraged me on this path. KRISHNAMURTI, of whom Deepak Chopra said, "He made it possible for me to break through the confines of my own self-imposed restrictions to my freedom"; and a brilliant Aldous Huxley using almost exactly the same language.

And the other giant thinker was the Federal Judge LEARNED HAND... who in his career never had one word of an opinion changed by the U.S. Supreme Court.

My own thoughts were these before being encouraged by the writings of the two men mentioned. A most meaningless cliché is "moderation in all things". Moderation is the key to mediocrity. Moderation is defined as: "staying within accepted limits." Creative and uncommon people who are memorable and who use their time on this Earth to the fullest are usually most immoderate and never stay within the accepted limits.

The Sadducees and the Pharisees stayed within the accepted limits of Hebrew law. Jesus did neither. He immoderately loved those whom the Pharisees despised, and he immoderately shattered a great many of their rules and traditions. The most creative giants of civilization, in all disciplines, have forgotten themselves into immortality by vast immoderate creativity and contributions and by never "staying within accepted limits."

4

Our obsession with outside "authority", whether in institutions or individuals, ensures that we remain emotionally and spiritually dwarfed as children. Human beings, in the mass, sink unconsciously to an inferior moral and intellectual level. Human beings, in the mass, like sheep, obeying and following the "accepted limits" of outside authorities end up as zeros as individuals who never listen to their inner voice...their inner intuition... their own reason. The tragedy of this for society is that a million zeros joined together add up to.....ZERO, and not even to one.

I turned from my thinking to Krishnamurti who wrote: "*CONVENTION leads to MEDIOCRITY. Conventional education makes independent thinking extremely difficult. We are turning out, as if through a mold, a type of human being whose primary interest is to find security...to become important, or to have a good time with as little thought as possible. Conventional education puts an end to spontaneity and breeds fear. It is this fear that kills the spirit. Our entire upbringing and education have made us afraid to be different from our neighbor, and to think contrary to the established pattern of society, falsely respectful of authority and tradition. Highly awakened intelligence is INTUITION, which is the only true guide in life.*"

I can tell you, in all truth, that years ago, 50 to be exact, it was the brilliant essays of Federal Judge LEARNED HAND that encouraged me to choose the path of independent thinking. This awesome thinker had no superior in the jurisprudence of the English-speaking world. I discovered his book THE SPIRIT OF LIBERTY....The Addresses of LEARNED HAND...Alfred A. Knopf....1960. And in those essays I found my north star... my directions for my life's path. I find these words brilliant, eloquent and profound, "*We pour our libations to our traditions, long after they have ceased to mean what they once did.*"

5

"My thesis is that any organization of society which depresses doubting and controversy, along with free and spontaneous meddling is on the decline. Liberty is gone, little as its members may know it. Once you get people believing that there is an authoritative well of wisdom to which they can turn for absolutes, you have dried up the springs. As soon as we cease to pry about, to doubt, question and challenge, we shall come to rely upon accredited bodies of authoritative dogma; and as soon as we come to rely upon accredited bodies of authoritative dogma, not only are the days of our Liberty over, but we have lost the password of freedom and truth that has hitherto opened to us the gates of freedom.

If you accept this it will cast you in the role of Prometheus… whose role was defying the Powers of the World. Your audience may be very small; indeed, it is possible that there will be none at all. But the lead is a man's part, and perhaps some of us can fill it...."

These thoughts, among others, are the true heart of my reflections as I look back over my 90 years....and the "true path" (as the Lakota say) of my life. I would do nothing differently. From Marine Corps pilot flying, to University teaching, to reflective groups of Symposium thinkers.....it has been a good, productive and creative trip. And my doctor told me last week that I have at least another good ten to go and he would bet that I easily will hit..........100. At that age, I will write you again…about "reflections at 100." Stay tuned.

THE MOON OF THE NEW GRASS

My brothers and sisters of the Lakota and Cheyenne people called this time of year in their calendric system, "the moon of the new grass....new life...new renewal". They knew this, naturally, living so close to the rhythms of the natural world.

Within those rhythms we are moving now into the month of March, of new grass, new life and new renewals. I have my calendar of the soul that is far more accurate than the printed one on my desk. It tells me that nature says the new year is here, with bursting buds and warm earth and fresh new leaves dancing and quaking on bare winter branches.

I am not alone in calling this "moon of the new grass" and renewal the beginning of my new year. The ancient Jews, Egyptians and Greeks all had early March as the beginning.

It is the time of year when "Hyla crucifer" begins to call. The little peeper makes a calculation which would baffle a meteorologist. He takes into consideration humidity, temperature, length of light and darkness, and knows when the rhythm of renewal has come. He inflates a little bubble in his throat and sends out a clear note audible for half a mile. At that point, something older than any mythological god has risen. THE EARTH IS ALIVE AGAIN. ALIVE, with new grass, new life, new beginnings.

Where is it that I most fully experience this glorious new time of the earth coming to life? For the entire twenty years of my full time residence in Palm Springs, I have never been able to say "thank you" enough for the glorious gift of the sacred canyons of the Cahuilla Indians as a spiritual retreat that truly "transcends language." When you drive through the gate and enter a magical and mystical world of the sacred earth .....with no fences....no telephone poles....no visual pollution.....and go sit by the stream.....with the tranquil sounds of water bubbling and trickling....you can rewind...REWIND your mind/ brain/

7

soul/spirit back into another timeframe. Where the flow and rhythms of the universe, the seasons of the new leaves quaking over new grass...the seasons of spring and fall equinox, the winter and summer solstice and the times of the full moon still nurture the land, the four-leggeds and two-leggeds, the feathered ones of the air...raven...and red tailed hawk.... and everything and all that has evolved from the same FIRST SOURCE.

In Zen Buddhism they say that "*the highest modes of experience transcend the reach of any language*" And so it is. How can I, through words, describe what I feel in the desert rain? The fragrant odors…the rich aroma of an earth moist and alive. Rolling sounds of thunder waking the earth from its restful slumber, as they say in the Taos Pueblo, followed by dazzling rainbows receiving a standing ovation from the little red flames on the tip of the Ocotillos. And the Candle of the Lord, the eloquent creamy white blossoms shooting up high on their great spike of the Yucca.

When sitting on a rock slab, in the midst of all of these miracles of the natural world in the Indian Canyons, I always find joy in letting my mind and emotions play with deep and significant questions. How is it that we are all connected in some marvelous and mysterious way to this cosmic dance of solstice and equinox? This something unknown doing we know not what. I am in awe gazing at the wild flowers. A long, long time ago, there were no flowers. And then, just before the Age of Reptiles, there was a soundless explosion that lasted over a million years. It was the emergence of the angiosperms, the flowering plants. And from these flowers came the mystifying emergence of man. The flowers have a long memory in their seeds, and I too, as I remember that my very existence as Homo sapiens depends on these flowers.

And I think that the flowers of a rainy Spring, and the grasses of a showery Summer are good and beautiful and sufficient, even though they will shortly vanish.

Here in the Indian Canyons, I live surrounded by miracles, and I realize that we humans are only a very small part, a unit of one, symbiotically related and dependent upon all the other billions of protoplasmic relatives.

The Canyons remind me that we must come to terms with non-physical reality. We came from non-physical reality and we will return to non-physical reality, two realities which are yet ONE. Every moment of our lives we are being influenced by other energies from non-physical realities. It is like ultraviolet light, microwave light and infrared light and many other ranges of frequencies which coexist with our visible light spectrum and yet are invisible to us. Solstice and Equinox remind me that we live in the midst of and are supported by mysteries beyond our comprehension. "*This Mystery*" as Albert Einstein wrote "*that is the source of all true art and true science.*"

The desert speaks to me of endurance and flexibility, silence and solitude. The living forms of the four-legged and the two-legged, the winged ones of the air and the crawling ones on the ground adjust to the heat of the day and cold of the night. And the great, lush oasis of the desert canyons remind us of the Yin and Yang of nature and how it cares for its own. Long after our artificial cities have crumbled....the desert, with its timeless beauty, will once again call to those who have survived.

When confused and fragmented by city chaos, perhaps it is in the desert, and the precious gem of the Indian Canyons, that in silence and solitude we find our spiritual oasis.

Having personally experienced a recent major "LIFE RENEWAL" with a new aortic heart valve...driving out again to the Canyons several days ago....I sat by that sacred water....in that sacred place....with soft light flickering through the palm leaves. I had once again to just throw up my hands

9

to the sacred and mystical presence of WAKAN TANKA, the great MYSTERY of the Lakota and Cheyenne, the Mystery who gave these precious and magnificent INDIAN CANYONS to the Cahuilla.....who have allowed us to share in their grandeur and gift to our sense of wonder, awe, and balance. To that same Mystery...who is a presence and protector of many Indian traditions........I threw up my hands.......and offered a verbal affirmation of......THANK YOU......to the Mystery and to the Cahuilla..... THANK YOU.

A thought....for your meditation: Spiritual consciousness is our being.. the context of life itself. Expanding consciousness is always a risky business....for it endangers the vested interests of the status quo.

WHAT DOES IT MEAN TO BE HUMAN?

The scene is always the same. I have been introduced and the time has come for me to speak. I step up to the rostrum and look out into the faces turned toward me. And often from each unique flower of a face, I see the stem that winds out of the auditorium door… back into their homes… out into the backyard, only to vanish down into the earth. The stem winds back two million… five million… and even 100 million years. That is what we call them: "years." The odor of a far away pool comes into my head and there, in that pool, some cloudburst…some steaming water…some electrical storm gave forth life. I am aware of the stem that stretches behind the flower of my face, back to the dark of a leaf fall, back to something that slunk under the glitter of a glacial night that roamed under a moon of many ice ages. And I stand there, as the "sapiens" animal at this end of the stem in this small point of eternal time.

As we enter a New Year I am asking, "What does it mean to be human?" If some million or so years ago you had gazed around you at your fellow creatures with a sense of unease and said, "Ah, at last this is what it means to be human" you would have been wrong.

Had you gazed at Olduvai Gorge man and said, "Yes, now this is what it means to be human," you would have been wrong. For that creature was not "man" but only an upright creature in a moment of time, in the unfolding, evolving process of change, and it did not yet appear what it would become.

If 150,000 years ago you had looked at your Neanderthal brothers and sisters and said, "Ah, now at last, this is what it means to be human," you would have been wrong.

You could have been a sensitive artist of 20,000 years ago in a Cro-Magnon cave, who squinted through the smoke of a sputtering torch, and rose from that rubbled floor and decorated your ceiling with works of beauty that have endured for over 20,000 years. It is a sermon in stone. The creative spark cannot be extinguished. But had you gazed around that cave and said, "Ah, now at last, finally this is what it means to be human" you would have been wrong.

These were what we call "pre-historic" days. But you see, you must not ever forget, that we, you and I, are also "pre-historic." And if you will take the time to look around you today at those other creatures called "Homo sapiens" you will probably say, "Ah, now, at last, finally, this is what it really means to be human." And, of course, as in the past million years, you will be so very, very wrong. For there is always an invisible doorway ahead, which, in a continual process of change and unfolding, takes us beyond the nature that we know.

Our Neanderthal and Cro-Magnon relatives were playing a part in a play that they knew very little about. What is exciting to me is that today, you and I are playing a leading part on a vast stage in this unfolding drama of evolution and creation.

We are active participants in contributing an answer to the question of what it means to be human. What a grand drama we are playing out, to be able to make choices that transcend genetic and environmental influences and thus enter into the continuing process of creation.

"*The evolution of our spirit,*" wrote Bertrand Russell, "*is blazed on the dark background of eternity by our individual wakes. Every person can, if he/she wishes, leave a more or less brilliant wake behind them, which widens or prolongs the existing path and contributes to the fanlike expansion.*"

We WILL leave a wake behind us in this New Year of 2011 ahead. The spirit of our species is evolving, an evolution of consciousness. Will the wake we leave behind us make a difference in our understanding of all that it means to be human and humane?

It is we, ourselves, who can give our lives and our wake a significance that transcends death.

THE WAKE WE LEAVE BEHIND

Ages ago... ages and ages ago... a wandering star passed too near the sun... and drew out from it by its gravitational pull this planet... that ever since has swung around its solar center, has gradually cooled off, given birth to life and become the habitat of our strange... strange human race. What does it all mean?

We live in a world of ideas, ideals, intellect, conscience, creative genius, faith, hope, love. AND what does it all mean?

And when we ask those questions, whether in a scientific laboratory, a church sanctuary, in a flower-blanketed alpine meadow, alone at the top of a snowy slope with only the silence... or in a moment of private meditation and introspection. Wherever those questions are asked that have to do with meaning, and the mystery of existence and eternal things... that is where the spiritual reaches its most profound dimensions. The person asking and seeking their most sacred moments, experiencing the mystical dimensions of reality.

Two of our most beautiful people who had experienced this spiritual reality were Charles and Ann Lindberg. If you have not read Ann Lindberg GIFT FROM THE SEA... do read it. I have lost count of the dozens of times that I have read it and used it.

But what few know is about her husband Charles. He could live in the visible world of flying and testing fighter planes in the South Pacific in WWII, for marine and navy pilots, but what few know is that he constantly lived too in the invisible world of mystical experience. In 1953 in the book THE SPIRIT OF ST. LOUIS he writes of transcending space and time... remembrance of other lives, loss of fear of death and a lasting shift of values in his life.

14

He wrote that in the eighteenth hour of his flight, "*I felt myself as an awareness of spreading through space... over the earth and into the heavens... unhampered by time or substance. The fuselage behind me filled with presences.. outlined forms.. transparent.. moving.. riding with me in the plane.. weightless. I saw them around me as though my skull was one great eye. They talked with me.. giving me answers to my navigational problems.. giving me information of importance.. unattainable in ordinary life. I was one with them. I felt no weight in my body. I was in a greater realm beyond.. caught in a field of gravitation between two planets. I felt power incomparably stronger than anything that I have ever known. The presences around me were like a gathering of family and friends.. long separated.. as though we all had known one another in some part incarnation. Death no longer seemed the final end that it used to be for me, but rather the entrance to a new and free existence. The values and priorities of my life changed radically following that flight and that experience.*"

Now those are not the words of some flake coming off the wall. That was the experience of so committed and dedicated and objective a scientist as Charles Lindberg.

Fifty years later when he lay dying in his cottage in Hawaii his wife asked him to share with her the experience of confronting the end. "What was it like to face death?" she asked him. "There is nothing to face," he answered.

People within the so called NEW AGE (Aquarius) orientation are more and more moving away from the doctrines and dogmas of orthodoxy... to the beauty of direct spiritual experience. They are coming together in groups of kindred spirits who share this understanding, this vision and this quest. And share with the great Christian mystic of the 13th century Meister Eckhart these words, "*The more people are free of all things and turn to themselves, the more they will know in themselves.. know all things clearly without any*

15

hindrance from outside. The more they do this the more they are truly human…"

"The eye in which I see God is the same eye in which God sees me. My eye and God's eye are one eye. There is only one eye… one seeing… one knowing… one loving…"

Two people come to the end of this life on earth. Their findings and reports of what they saw will be different. Both have eyes, but they have been headed in different emotional and spiritual directions. They both will have passed through the same life on the same earth, in the same town, but they will not have seen the same thing nor known the same joys; for they have had two different perspectives and destinations. One has seen life as something waiting to be endured... as meaningless. Another has seen life as a glorious drama played on a majestic stage.

It is all a matter of perspective… of perspective. It's good to remember that when people say, "Nothing changes," they are usually either talking about their little 70 years of the view, or else our little 7,000 years of what we call civilization. AND good heavens… what a narrow perspective… trying to see the total 8 billion year history of the planet from our little 70 or 7,000 year span!

Things do change. The spirit of our species is evolving as more and more individuals like you and me harmonize our lives with our creative spirit so that our individual wakes, even like the wake of a pebble dropped in a pool of water, extend out, fanlike… further and further.

A little ant walking through gravel sees gigantic white and black boulders. You and I look down and see little gravel. From a different perspective, flying at 40,000 feet, we are ant hills. I think the perspective that we are or may be evolving spiritually and ethically even though it seems against the current is not invalid.

Well if while we are on the stage we feel that we are traveling toward lightness rather than darkness, it makes all the difference. Whether we are stumbling toward an endless abyss or toward an eternal destiny... When you believe that the path upwards ends in meaning, it makes a difference in the living of these days. And even though history is full of wars and detours, to believe that we always come back to the main highway... makes a difference.

I'll tell you how I feel. Maybe some of you feel the same way, too. I look at this incomprehensible, indifferent universe, and I look at my brief years on the stage as an actor in the play. I don't want any cues or prompter behind the curtains telling me my lines, and where to stand, and where to walk, and when to sit, and when to get up. No. But rather on that stage I want to play the man's part and spontaneously say my own lines, and write in my own movements, and my own stage business, and play the part that is written for me by the author. And I WANT TO weave, while here, the surest fabric of myself. My audience may be very small. Indeed, I may have no audience and certainly no applause. But far more important, I will have played the part written for me.

There was a brilliant moment in history when a few took the stage and played their part well. They are called The AXIAL THINKERS. They left a wake still brilliant today.

In the words of Loren Eiseley, *"We suffer from a nostalgia for which there is no remedy except as it is to be found in the enlightenment of the spirit and consciousness. In the first millennium before Jesus... in the great centers of civilization whether Chinese, Indian, Judaic or Greek, the destiny of the human spirit became of more significance than the looting of a province."*

At that point there was a great period of light that Karl Jaspers refers to as the "period of the axial thinkers." Though the dreams and the hopes are expressed in different ways they share many aspirations and beliefs. The period of the creators of transcendent values founded the world of universal thought. That is our most precious human heritage. They mark a rejection of purely material goals; a turning toward some inner light. They did not come with weapons. They dreamed of creating a new and nobler human being.

The spiritual foundations of a new consciousness of humanity were laid almost simultaneously in China, India, Persia, Palestine and Greece. And these are the spiritual foundations upon which humanity still subsists today. Who were these people, the unknown authors of ancient Hindu scriptures, the Hebrew prophets, Confucius, Zoroaster, Buddha, Socrates, Plate, later Jesus and Mohammed. It was a period of blinding light, and we still live in its glow, in the wake, in its reflection. We who can, even now, reflect more of the light into the hopes and the dreams of a new tomorrow.

This period is a historical mystery. How can we explain how they came into existence across the land mass of Europe and Asia in such diverse cultures at roughly the same time? It was a period that opened up the human soul. It was a period flooded with light illuminating the way. One droplet joined another droplet. The spiritual evolution of our species is the same thing. Gravity pulls the water downhill. Is there a divine gravity that is pulling us and life up... up... onward toward some destiny? And as the droplet of one just life... of one just person is joined by another just person, and yet another, the momentum builds up in this evolving nature of our species.

This has been the pattern of life for millions of years, from shapeless matter to homo sapiens, thinking like man with a moral and ethical and spiritual conscience. What a wonderful drama in which we all have our parts to play. Some of us play our parts well. Some of us refuse to play, and some of us refuse to even come onto the stage.

Do you want to know something that excites me when I think about it? My cave man ancestors were playing a part in a play that they probably knew very little about. They did not understand too much about this life, but what excites me is that now you and I are playing our part on this stage with knowledge of the part we are playing. We understand the play much better and understand our roles in it, even though we choose to disregard it often times. The fact you cannot see where it is going is not important. The key phrase is "directions without destination and the wake we leave."

When I stop and think of the part I am playing in the drama then it gives my life purpose and destination. It is so easy you know to get down and discouraged regardless of how you spend your days. Who hasn't? Sometimes I think about my own days speaking and teaching and writing and words, words, words. I work for hours and days on a talk or lecture or speech that is over in 20 minutes or an hour. And I think, "So what?" Everyone back now to business as usual. But then I stop. I stop and place it in a larger perspective, a larger context and framework. I remember how Hitler in MEIN KAMPF using words for evil said in one hour of preaching he could change people 180 degrees. I remember the good words of a Churchill who did the same. I remember Queen Bloody Mary of Scotland saying she feared the preaching of John Knox more than all the armies that could be amassed against her. And I remember that lives and civilizations and history have been changed, altered, improved or destroyed through words, writing and speaking.

And then you see from this perspective my days take on a new dimension and a new significance, and I eagerly look forward to the next speech, or the next essay, and the next column and the next.

I am saying all of us can look at our days and place it in a larger context and meaningful framework, and give it eternal perspective as we see the part we are playing. "The evolution of our spirit is blazed on the dark background of eternity by our individual wakes. Every person can, if he/she wishes, leave a more or less brilliant trace behind which widens or prolongs the existing path and contributes to its fanlike expansion."

YOU are leaving a wake. That is reality. A wake, either destructive or constructive; positive or negative.

Well, if we have the courage it means to engage your community, your state, your world with creative courage… the creative courage of a Voltaire, an Erasmus and Meister Eckhart, a Bruno, a Galileo, the immortality of words and the writers who use those words that had been rubbed shiny. More people today are moved and inspired by Voltaire and Erasmus and Jefferson than in their own day. And they have more to say to us than any bulletin coming out of Cape Canaveral or Edwards Air Force Base.

It is true that not one of the religious figures really knew where he was going or his message… whether a Buddha, a Confucius, a Jesus, a Moses, Socrates or could possibly foresee the outcome of their lives and thought. Perhaps it is true in its most profound sense that a person never rises so high as when he/she takes creative risks. So when we come to the evolution of consciousness we are moving into one of the major revolutions of the new century, and it has to do with human choices. I repeat human choices and the impact and importance of human choices on ideas.

The evolution of human consciousness is hidden in quantum physics, and quantum physics is the brainchild of the brilliant genius Neils Bohr, who was and is as great as Einstein. Upon receiving the Nobel Prize Neils Bohr chose the Tai Chi disk as the special crest just for him and his family.

Science cannot explain spiritual experiences or extrasensory perception (Lindberg) or the evolution of consciousness, but the evolution of consciousness has obviously come about through human consciousness. A human being's main distinction from animals is that our consciousness stretches far, far beyond survival needs. We have only to look at art, music, literature, inventions to realize that Homo sapiens has always, through consciousness, wanted to reach far beyond survival necessities. Therefore, consciousness has existed prior to the creation of matter.

As one quantum physicist put it, *"To think of matter as ultimate is like saying, IF WE HAVE ENOUGH CHAIRS WE CAN FORM A COMMITTEE."*

The wake we will leave... what will it be? There was an artist in a cave who left a wake 20,000 years ago. He squinted through the smoke of a sputtering torch, rose from that rubbled floor and decorated that ceiling with works of beauty that have endured for 20,000 years. It is a sermon in stone... a wake. The creative spark cannot be extinguished. 20,000 years ago, in the midst of perilous times, the human spirit rose from this rubbled cave floor and brought beauty to a ceiling, through creative thought.

But do not forget that we today of this century, in a way, we are pre-history too; for the new ages of tomorrow. Let us ask, what light can we contribute? What beauty and threads of thought can we pass on in our own time?

IDEAS THAT USE US

When we look at creative lives, past and present, that have been made great by great ideas, it brings to us a very stimulating message, a challenging message. It is THAT YOU AND I NEED NOT BE VERY GREAT TO CHOOSE AND BE USED BY SOME VERY GREAT IDEAS. An inspiring message to us is that the wake we leave behind us as we live our days will be more significant and more monumental as our wake has been filled with some of the great ideas of civilization.

We are constantly being used by ideas and if we are not being used by great and noble ideas, we are being used by small, petty and trivial ideas.

In every generation the great ideas and the sick ideas must find human beings that they can use or they would die out. Generation after generation, human beings come and go, but ideas remain and words live on. Human beings die but ideas survive and knock on a living mind and say, "Let me use you now in your time."

So, the "bottom line," as they say, is this:

THE ULTIMATE MEANING OF OUR LIVES AS HUMAN BEINGS IS TO BE FOUND IN THE IDEAS THAT WE ALLOW TO USE US.

We magnetize into our lives and thinking whatever ideas we hold in our thoughts. In every generation the great ideas and the sick ideas must find a human mind that they can use or they would die. Human beings die but ideas and words survive.

Ideas are not a person's private property. They are historic. They cannot survive with a human being representing them. I hear a speaker put forth an idea, I read an idea in a book, and I say YES… YES I will represent you with my life and thought.

Thomas Jefferson approached death in bankruptcy. They made Socrates drink the hemlock. They died, but knowing that they had lived their lives to the fullest and had allowed only the greatest ideas to use their days on this earth. Jefferson said that when he wrote the Declaration of Independence, he had used the greatest ideas of civilization, known to him, to be included. But we do not have to be a Jefferson or Socrates to be used by great ideas. Water is represented not just be large lakes or an ocean, but water is represented also by brooks and small streams.
Being used by great ideas makes the wake we leave behind one of substance for those in its path. There is an immortality to the ideas we leave in our wake. There are more people today reading Lao Tzu, Buddha, Jesus, Meister Eckhart, Voltaire, Erasmus, Jefferson, the philosophers of Athens and Rome, than in their own time. The immortality of words and great ideas leaves a wake of gigantic importance and influence that widens and prolongs our human path and contributes to its fanlike expansion.

It is true that the more we associate with and read great and giant spirits, the more we are liberated from trivia.

We are being used by ideas every minute of every day and through those ideas that we allow to use us, we create the wake we leave behind us in this life as we approach our terminal point, our last living days.

But one truth remains clear and factual. WE HAVE MAGNETIZED INTO OUR LIVES THE WORDS AND THE THOUGHTS OF THE IDEAS WE HAVE ALLOWED TO USE US. You and I have had no need to be very great, to be used by great ideas.

THE SPIRIT WORLD

Over the course of my long life, there have been so many events that have influenced me, events that have been beyond comprehension, beyond explanation, far beyond the law of probability, and even beyond Carl Jung's "synchronicity."

It was my dear friend, Vine Deloria, Lakota Indian, distinguished scholar and author, who introduced me to the "spirit world." This was the subject of his last book, before he passed away and went on to "the other side" of the spirit world. He always told me he would communicate with me after he went to the "other side." He did. I will describe that later in the column, but first, thoughts about the "spirit world."

"Life," so called, is only a short interlude between two great mysteries which are yet ONE. Spring begins with winter and death begins with birth and we all share the same breath together in this short interlude of "life"…the trees, flowers, birds and animals, including the human animal. We all dance to a common rhythm.

We live in the midst of, and are supported by, mysteries beyond our comprehension.

We are ONE with our sacred earth, and we are also ONE with the furthest star in the furthest galaxy. We feel, we sense, that in some way, somehow, we are all together, "dancing to a whispered voice overheard by the soul." As you study the images of the Eagle Nebula, brought back by the Hubble Telescope from deep space where stars are born, it is easy to imagine the interplay of Cosmic forces, across space and time, of matter and spirit, dancing to the music of the spheres.

Spirit merges with matter to sanctify the Universe. The star-lit magic of the OUTERmost life of our Universe becomes the soul-light magic of the INNERmost life of our self. The energy of the stars becomes US. We become the energy of the stars. Stardust and Spirit unite and we are ONE with the Universe, Whole from ONE source, endless creative energy bursting forth as we, the earth, air, water and fire have burst forth from over fifteen billion years of Cosmic energy. It does not require any imagination to realize the very active presence of the spirit world in our everyday world of earth living.

We must come to terms with non-physical realities. It is like light… ultraviolet light… microwave light… and infrared light and many other ranges of frequencies which coexist with our visible light spectrum, and yet are invisible to us. How many other non-physical energy frequencies co-exist with us and yet are invisible?

Out of hundreds, I have chosen only two examples from my own life of contact with the spirit world.

When I was the minister of the Community Congregational Church in McCall, Idaho, a resort town in the mountains of central Idaho, my 85 year-old mother died. She loved being in this very liberal church every Sunday morning.

The next Sunday, after she passed over, I was sitting in my study. The choir (about 25 people) was practicing on the chancel. I heard a shot, much like a rifle shot. I ran out into the sanctuary to see what happened and found the chancel completely covered with a white foam-like substance, not a liquid, and fairly solid. The choir members were all in a state of shock. The custodians and choir members started looking everywhere to see where it came from; the walls were all solid… the roof… they even went up on either side of the chancel where the organ pipes were, and found NOTHING. Walls with no crack. Ceiling with no crack. Nobody EVER had a clue as to the source of that foam. With broom and vacuum it was finally cleaned up. The choir and I told the congregation that morning that "my mother paid us a visit this morning."

One more example: Vine Deloria told me he would contact me if possible, after he went into the "spirit world." He did. On the night of November 11, I lectured at the Santa Barbara City College, a Friday night. Two days later, November the 13th, the publisher and editors of the NewsPress paper invited me and my wife to lunch with them at one of the most popular places on the ocean. I write for that paper. That morning, Sunday, the 13th, Vine Deloria went to the "other side" in Golden, Colorado. I had been told he passed on. We were having lunch at noon that day, about 80 or more people on the patio. After lunch, about 1:30, everyone at our table got up to leave. My wife waited for me and I followed very shortly. As I was walking out, I felt a tug on my arm and turned around. There was an Indian woman standing there with a little, maybe 2 year-old daughter in her arms. She said to me "I am so sorry to bother you, but for the last 15 minutes my little daughter has been pointing at you and saying 'touch… touch.' She has never done that before." Please remember there were around 80 people on the patio so I was not that visible or prominent. The little girl kept touching my arm and laughing and smiling from ear to ear. The mother thanked me. As we walked on to the car, I said to my wife "that was Vine." When I got back to our motel, I called his widow in Golden, Colorado. She cried.

There is no dualism. There are not two worlds or two dimensions of reality: One where we live on this earth, and Two, the spirit world of those who have gone on to the "other side." There is only ONE reality, and "Life," so called, is only a brief interlude between two great mysteries, which are yet… ONE."

The American Indian has known this for thousands of years. Many in our culture, are just now getting the message and the truth of this insight, an insight that changes your life.

MYSTICISM – THE PATH TO TRUTH

In this column, I want to think and reflect on a word that is misunderstood by so many. That word is "mysticism."

What is mysticism? Mysticism is not sitting in a cave contemplating your navel. You can be a "mystic" and be working in the busiest office in downtown Chicago or San Francisco. In fact, it might save you from a lot of high blood pressure and migraine headaches if you were. Mysticism goes back as far as we can trace, in all religious traditions, including Judaism and Christianity. Experience and intuition are the two key words in mysticism. Wisdom, truth, insights are best discovered through intuition and experience. There is an inner knowledge that is not the result of an intellectual process. The mystic does not ignore reason and the intellect but knows that there is a limit to both. Where reason and intellect end, intuition takes over. The mystic goes beyond the obvious and the immediate and realizes that there is something more, something not visible, that there is an invisible world of realities, and truth, that can be discerned only through a leap of intuition.

The mystical orientation, or experience, is always the same, whether Taoist, Hindu, Native American, Buddhist, Christian or what have you. The mystic always points toward the **oneness**, the **wholeness** of the universe of which we are only a very small part. The word "God" is only a symbol for that Mystery that saturates and permeates everything in the universe. As the giant 13th century Christian mystic, Meister Eckhart, put it: "To watch a child pouring water into a glass is to watch God pouring God into God." Or again: "Going around looking for God is like sitting on an ox looking for an ox to ride." Or again: "The dung in the stable and God are One. The flea and God are One. Do you want to see God? Look into a mirror."

William James, the distinguished psychologist wrote: "*The mystic has insights into depths of truth that are unplumbed by the discursive intellect.*"

As Carl Jung put it: "*The creative mystic has always been a thorn in the side of the dogmatic and creedal church. But it is to the mystic that we owe all that is best in religion and humanity.*" It usually amazes people, when I am lecturing on this subject, to hear that a vast majority of our Nobel Prize-winning physicists are mystics. As theoretical physicists, they have, by intuition, seen into the nature of reality that goes far beyond the intellect. Mysticism and physics are fraternal twins. Albert Einstein wrote this: "*The cosmic order can be directly apprehended by the soul in the mystical union.*"

Today's physicists and quantum mechanics confirm that the archaic classifications of organic and inorganic, animate and inanimate, do not exist and are invalid. Of course, the Eastern spiritual traditions, the Native Americans and mystics of all time and place have known this for thousands of years. What this belief says is: *Everything is One. The Mystery within us is the same Mystery that is in every leaf, every atom, every molecule.* The Cosmos is everything. The Cosmos is the totality of all things. You cannot experience God, for you are already It. God and a cucumber are One. God and the flea are One. The wolf, the dragonfly and I, we are One. An old Chinese text reads: "*There is no Creator. Everything produces itself and is not produced by others. This is the natural way of the Universe.*" Modern physicists would say, "Yes, they knew what they were talking about." There is only creativity and it is constantly going on. It is a continuous process, and everything is alive and in movement, even though invisible to the naked eye. We are a part of the cosmic dance. Life is a dance and the dance goes on in time and space.

A text of second century Judaism says: "*God is not **external** to anything in the universe. All is One with the One as the flame is one with the candle.*" (Bear in mind, that is **second**

century Judaism). Life, so called, is only a short span between two great mysteries which are yet One. Fall begins with Spring, and Winter begins with Summer, and so-called death begins with birth, and it is all One and all interrelated.

What a dreamer am I. My dream: What a blessing it would be if all the religions that are based on dogmas, creeds and doctrines would give them up and become mystical. It is dogmas and doctrines that cause all of the hatred, violence and bloodshed. What a peaceful and harmonious world it would be, with the mystic philosophy. Ah, what a dreamer am I.

2000 YEARS OF DISBELIEF

I ask this question raised by Carl Jung: "Why are so many millions of people willing and eager to turn their lives over to outside authorities?" Why are so many today willing to turn their mind/brain…soul/spirit over to outside individuals, institutions and ideologies, whether it be Jewish, Muslim or Christian "authorities" of dogma? Or whatever the outside authority might be that is telling you what to think, what to believe and how to live your life.

I ask then, how do we withdraw from such a childish dependency if we want to reclaim our mind/brain and our very own life? I answered this by saying that first you must begin by taking a long, hard critical look at all so called religious authorities wanting to control your life, and be willing to accept the risk that goes with such courage and independence.

Our first six presidents had the courage to do that. American history scholars, writing for the Encyclopedia Britannica, have stated that our first six presidents were Deists and not Christian. I quote: "*One of the most embarrassing problems for the nineteenth-century champions of the Christian faith was the fact that not one of the first six presidents of the United States was a Christian. They were Deists.*" (1968, vol 2 p.420, Mortimer J. Adler, editor in chief. *The Annals of America: Great issues in American Life: A Conspectus*)

Thomas Jefferson used these words to express his view: "*On the dogmas of religion, all mankind, from the beginning of the world to this day, have been quarreling, fighting, burning and torturing one another, for abstractions unintelligible to themselves and to all others, and absolutely beyond the comprehension of the human mind.*" (Jefferson to Carey in 1816, ms 1V)

One of the most valuable books in my library, and one I have reviewed many times, that will make a monumental contribution toward historical and religious literacy is *2000 Years of Disbelief, Famous People With The Courage to Doubt* by James Haught, published by Prometheus Books. James Haught is the Executive Editor of the Charleston Gazette. He has received many honors and awards from the National Press Club, the American Bar Association, and People For The American Way.

The book profiles the giants of history, in many vocations and disciplines, and their challenge to the religious "authorities" of their day and to Christianism in general. They took charge of their own mind/brains and of their own life. With every quote in the book revealing their beliefs, you are told exactly where you can find the statement if you doubt the accuracy of it. You can look it up yourself.

Those with constipated minds, of course, will never take the time to pursue the subject and become accurately informed. Our first six presidents, as well as many others, are well covered in the book. It brings together the words of the great minds of both East and West, from antiquity to the present. It is an anthology of outstanding philosophers, scientists, poets, scholars and politicians, as well as giants of the arts.

As a sourcebook of those who took charge of their own mind/brain and challenged the Christian and religious tyranny of their day, it is priceless. The book will lead the open and enlightened mind into a greater depth of study. The book will bring to your attention, once more, the myth and fantasy of the religious and political right wing stating that this nation was founded by Christians and the bible. That brainwashing propaganda will be seen for the fallacy it is.

Thomas Jefferson put in one succinct sentence what they all believed: "*The day will come when the mystical generation of Jesus, by a supreme being as his father in the womb of a virgin, will be classed with the fable of the generation of*

Minerva in the brain of Jupiter." (Letter to John Adams, April 11, 1823)

In how many ways do we let outside "authorities" take over our mind/brain to the total exclusion of facts? How many, without question, accept moss-covered clichés fed to us by religiously and historically illiterate speakers and columnists on local and national levels? A perfect example is a national column by Kathleen Parker, writing in her *USA Today* essay. She proclaimed, in her most ignorant and authoritative way, that, "*There were no atheists in the World Trade Center on September 11, even as there are never any atheists in foxholes.*"

What hogwash! What nonsense! In my twelve years of flying as a U.S. Marine Corps pilot in both WWII and Korea, I knew many, I repeat MANY, Marines who were atheists and had nothing to do with God talk, Jesus talk or Bible talk.

Easily, one of the most valuable two weeks of my time spent at the University of Colorado had nothing to do with Anthropology, but was when Dr. John Greenway used two weeks to teach critical reading and thinking.

Of course, everything we have been thinking about in this column was the major emphasis with the Buddha 2,500 years ago. He said again and again, "*Be ye lamps unto yourselves.*" Do not accept tradition or any outside authority, for these are the chains that bind the human mind and spirit.

For those wanting such a freedom and the joys that go with that freedom, I think you will find this book *2000 Years of Disbelief* a treasure that you will read again and again. It will give you the latitude and longitude of the courage it takes to free the mind.

The advance of Western Civilization has been the story of the gradual victory of free thought over the dogma and tyranny of religion.

LIFE IS PARADOX

A balanced life demands that we hold in a creative tension what seem to be logical contradictions. We all live, hourly and daily, with the paradoxes that are a part of every decision, the paradoxes within us. You cannot read the biographies of any brilliant man or woman without realizing what a mass of contradictions and complex personalities they were, and yet still, the creativity that flowed from their lives left a wake far and wide that influenced all in its path... Churchill and Jefferson, Jung and Einstein, Bohr and O'Keeffe and on through them all. We hold the paradoxes of our lives in a balanced creative tension leading to a stable and productive existence.

Most of us live by some "system" of thought. It can be a philosophical system, an economic system, a theological system, a morality system, and to try to live by any one system, and make an absolute out of it, is to imprison the human spirit.

Systems are always needing to be opened up to let out the soul and spirit of a unique human being. Because no ONE system has the handle for truth. Truth is always beyond. As Neils Bohr put it: *"every truth has an opposite, a paradox, that is also a great truth."*

Every "system" is only a fragment, a minute particle, a pebble on the cosmic beach of truth. And any one system contradicts another system, or negates another system, and other dimensions and other realities as well as other truths are always beyond.

Systems of thought become strait jackets, binding us and imprisoning us as we try to make every idea and every part of life fit into our system, no matter how we have to twist it, bend it, pervert it, force it. We mutilate history, knowledge and facts to force them into our system of thought that we have turned

34

into an absolute. For instance, there is no one system that can explain a human being. Not genetics, psychology, medicine, home values, or any other system of thought and theory and speculation, and no ONE system really tells you anything too important in any absolute way about the TOTAL YOU. Why? Because LIFE IS PARADOX.

And there lies the failures of "systems," the failure of any ONE system of thought. We must live daily, continually balancing between logic and the failure of logic… judgment and mercy… foolishness and wisdom… personal and social considerations… sorrow and joy… rest and action… prudence and carelessness… humility and confidence… the contemporary and timeless… weakness and strength… despair and hope… the mind and the heart… the old and new… tension and peace… love and indifference… life and death, and the PARADOXES PROVIDE THE BALANCE. When we balance the paradoxes in our lives we discover happiness due to an acceptance of the paradoxes.

Once you try to make an absolute or an ethical principle out of one side of a paradox, you have taken a virtue and turned it into a vice.

Take MERCY for instance, certainly a virtue, but if mercy is not checked by justice than mercy becomes a gushy, mushy, sentimental thing.

Take HUMILITY, a virtue I am sure, but if humility is not balanced by a strong and firm ego, a feeling of self respect and a sense of worth, then humility becomes a mealy-mouth thing, a crawling thing that no one can admire or respect.

Take THRIFT, a virtue no doubt, but when a person accumulates wealth and yet moans about how he "cannot afford" things that would bring pleasure and happiness, he has taken a virtue and turned it into a vice.

As soon as you try to make an absolute out of any ethical principle, then you have taken a seeming virtue and transformed it into a vice.

Life is beyond LOGIC… SYSTEMS… ABSOLUTES… for LIFE IS PARADOX, and there is no ONE handle that you can turn on to pour out happiness for you.

> I will be thinking in paradoxes… because life is.
> I will be teaching in paradoxes… because life is.
> I will be speaking in paradoxes… because life is.
> I will be acting in paradoxes… because life is.

That giant of thought, Waldo Emerson, said it well and eloquently: *"With consistency, a great and creative mind simply has nothing to do."*

As soon as we accept the fact that life is paradox, and that we live every hour of every day with paradoxes in a kind of creative tension, then we discover a new source of enormous energy that gives a significance to our days.

WHICH GOD?

From time to time, as do all writers, I receive anonymous letters. In some of these I have been asked, "Why do you always quote only men and women? Why don't you read the bible and quote God, where truth is?" That always reminds of a great cartoon in the *New Yorker* magazine. A minister is standing, robed, in his pulpit, with waving arms and saying, *"And now, reading from the bible, God says, and I quote of course…"*

Which "God" of the last 50,000 years do they want me to quote? Yahweh, Elohim, Ahura, Mazda, Ra, Osiris, Zeus, Jupiter, Dionysius, Demeter, Asklepios, Hermes, Aton, Odin, Thor, Varuna, Shang-ti, Amaterasu – Omikami, and we have not even touched the Goddesses.

OH NO, it is only biblical Gods that these writers are interested in, so again I would ask them, "Which 'biblical God' do they want me to quote, 'Yahweh, Elohim, Hadad, El Shaddai, Ba'alim or Anath'?

Or maybe the anthropomorphic "God" who walked and talked in the garden; or the "God" in Genesis who came down from the mountain to sire children by earth women (what a deal), or the jealous and vindictive God, the God of war, the vicious and cruel God who commanded a scorched earth and genocide, or the God in the Book of Numbers who commanded a young woman to be raped?

Even now, there are still some who believe that the bible is "infallible," "without error," the "word of God"…this God they want me to quote. Which story would I use for moral and spiritual edification? The inspirational story about Lot's two daughters who got him drunk with wine and went to bed with him? (Genesis 19) Today, we call it incest. You could call it holy debauchery I guess, since it is God's infallible "word." Well more of God's "word": There is the rape of Tamar by her brothers (2 Samuel) or a little gang rape in the Book of Judges (19-25). The "word of God" says "they abused her all the night long until the morning."

Thomas Paine, who gave us the name of The United States of America wrote, "Any system of religion that has anything in it that would shock the mind of a child cannot be a true system." Can any thoughtful person, say with honesty and integrity, that the majority of biblical concepts of "God" are not an insult to contemporary knowledge and spirituality?

It has been, and is, an uphill fight against narrow superstitions, antiquated religious doctrines and dogmas, combined with biblical illiteracy. We ask, "How could they have believed those asinine things?" Tragically, millions do. And still, when people die, millions still say, "God's will." In the magnificent words of the Rig-Vedas: "*Thou, before whom all words recoil, only silence can name thee.*"

THE TRUE BELIEVER

We seem to be living in a world of chaos, including our nation's capitol where the U.S. government is about to be shut down by the feuding political parties. What is the SOURCE of this chaos? THE TRUE BELIEVER is behind it all and promoting it due to the constipated mentality that lives in his head.

The mentality of the 'true believer' is exactly the same, whether Muslim, Christian, assorted versions of fundamentalism or any other religious beliefs… or fanatical political, racial or nationalistic dogmas. They are all alike and beyond rationality. Any attempt at calm and intelligent conversation will fail. That crackpot mentality does not want conversation but wants only to hear you say how wrong you are and how correct he is. He is a fanatic, needing a Stalin (or Jesus) to worship and die for.

I have had multiple experiences of this fact with Christian "born again" fundamentalists. They have told me they do not want to hear anything or read anything that is going to upset, or challenge, their locked in "belief" …no matter how factual. They have never realized how much unbelief is necessary to make belief possible. They do not have or want any understanding of their "belief"… they only need to believe.

A perfect example: in a study group that I had in Idaho, I was going through some of the great writings of Christian mystics, like Meister Eckhardt, who wrote: *"to see God, look in the mirror,"* or *"God is in the pile of dung in the stable,"* as well as other writings. A friend of mine said, *"Bill, I can't come to this group anymore and listen to these writings. I don't want to think about these things. I only want to believe what I believe."*

People who live in this frozen mentality of "belief" can always have the ground cut out from under them by any new discovery of science and scholarship and knowledge. Look what Galileo did to those who built their entire lives on an archaic "belief" system.

You want ignorant and illiterate "true believers"? There you are. And we are surrounded by them, by the millions.

The fanatic is perpetually incomplete and insecure. Reason does not faze him, nor does informed and intelligent communication.

The "true believer" always has to have an enemy. With Christian fundamentalists, the "enemies" are those educated, liberal Christians. With far-right House Republicans today it is Obama and the Democrats, whereas they have said, they "will do anything to embarrass Obama."

We have it from Hitler that the genius of a great leader consists in concentrating all hatred on a single foe. When told he was making the Jews too important, he responded, *"no...no...no. It is impossible to exaggerate the quality of the Jew as an enemy."*

Christianity was born, not by anything Jesus did, but on the end of the bloody sword of Constantine, a "true believer" who wanted state power. Martin Luther, a true believer, told the aristocracy in the Peasant Uprising, *"to cut the throat of a peasant will get you in heaven faster than prayer."*

John Calvin, a true believer, had people who opposed him burned at the stake.

The world has been drowning in the blood of the opponents of the "TRUE BELIEVER."

What a welcome blessing it will be for the world, when that day comes that a mature human mind accepts the truth that there are NO ABSOLUTES... and that in the words of Pascal, *"truth on this side of the mountain is falsehood on the other side of the mountain."*

Why? Because all truth is relevant to the mind that entertains it, and there are no absolutes. What is true and false, good and bad, is relevant to the individual mind and is NOT an absolute.

A delightful story from Taoism: What is good or bad depends upon whether you are a man, frog or mosquito. For the man, the frog is good as he can eat it, the mosquito is bad as it eats the man. For the frog, the man is bad and the mosquito good. For the mosquito, the frog is bad as it eats the mosquito, and the man is good to eat. So, what is good or bad depends upon whether you are a man, frog or mosquito. No absolutes.

All values are relative to the mind that entertains them.

What a beautiful day it will be for the world when, and if, the dogmatic and fanatic mind of the TRUE BELIEVER matures into the thought that… he could be wrong.

CULTS AND REAL RELIGION

Psycho-ceramic (crack pot) ideas sometimes spew out of politicians so fast it is almost impossible to keep up with them. The "faith-based" circus that totally destroys the line between church and state must be one of the most insane. Some of the TV evangelists have screamed "*You can't give money to cults… but only to real religion… like us…*"

Many have asked me the question: "What is a cult… and how can you tell the difference between a cult and a real religion?" Hey… easy question.

A Cult: Believes in heavenly signs such as comets and gateways to heaven and other mentally deranged ideas.

A Real Religion: Believes in heavenly signs such as stars in the East at their leaders birth and the "Sun standing still" for an entire day. (Joshua 10:12) and other mentally deranged ideas.

A Cult: Believes they have found the truth while all others are deceived.

A Real Religion: Believes they have found the truth while all others are deceived. "Salvation is only through Jesus."

A Cult: The leader says, "Believe me and you will go to heaven."

A Real Religion: The leader says, "Believe me and you will go to heaven. Don't believe me and you will go to someplace called hell."

A Cult: Has leaders, mostly men, often wearing fancy robes and promising you salvation and heaven if you will give them your money and property.

A Real Religion: Has leaders, mostly men, often wearing fancy robes and promising you salvation and heaven if you will give them your money and property.

A Cult: Claims their leader is led by God, and God speaks to him and tells him what to do. The leader talks to God.

A Real Religion: Claims their leader is led by God, and God speaks to him and tells him what to do. And the leader talks to God.

A Cult: Makes miraculous claims about the importance of their leader.

A Real Religion: Makes miraculous claims about their leader, that he was born of a virgin... could walk on water... could turn water into wine and feed thousands with only five loaves and two fish.

A Cult: Thinks women are subservient to men and the male leader and should take orders from them, including sexual bondage.

A Real Religion: Thinks women are subservient to men. "Let the women keep silence for it is not permitted for them to speak; they are commanded to be under obedience." (1Cor. 14:34) "Man was not created for the woman, but the woman for the man." (1Cor. 11:13) "Let women learn silence in all subjection. I suffer not a woman to have authority over a man." (1Timothy 2:11)

See how easy it is to tell a cult from a real religion? No problem.

Any individual on this little cosmic speck called Earth who really believes that he/she is speaking for the power behind a million galaxies in a universe beyond comprehension is closing in on insanity.

I was invited to speak a number of years ago to a state convention of Lutheran ministers in Tacoma, Washington. I asked them this question: "How many of you actually believe that you are speaking for a God of the universe when you are in the pulpit on a Sunday morning?" About three fourths of them held up their hand. I then said to them, "Not a one of you can explain a light bulb to me or a television set and yet you fantasize that you are speaking for the power behind the universe?" They never invited me back to speak again. I think you can see why.

In that classic university text book for religious studies, *The Ghost Dance*, the author Weston LaBarre of Duke University writes these words: "*The traditions of fundamentalist and orthodox Christianity give powerful support and impetus to cults, fantasies and fanaticism.*"

Concepts of a savior, authoritarian, father figure are appalling to Taoists, Buddhist, Zen Buddhist and Hindu. The pathology that goes with speaking for God, in this country at least, exists primarily in elements of Christianity.

There is a very, very thin, fine line between the Jim Jones's of the world and the Billy Graham's and Pat Robertson's… or any preacher who stands up in a pulpit and says… "*I am speaking for God… listen to me… I have the 'saving' words for you that are going to lead you into heaven… help me lead people into heaven… just send cash or checks to help me lead people to heaven…*"

Robert Ingersoll offers us a humorous final image. "*Can anyone really believe that God created this universe simply for the purpose of raising orthodox Christians? And that he is finally going to turn heaven into a religious museum filled with Baptist barnacles, petrified Presbyterians and Methodist mummies?*"

Do not miss this final word. There is a vast chasm between orthodox, institutionalized religion and spirituality. A human being can be profoundly spiritual without any attachment to doctrinal man-made systems.

THE PULPIT NEEDS AGNOSTICS

For more than 25 years the beloved Senior Minister of the famed City Temple of London (Methodist) was Leslie Weatherhead. His books have been read by millions.

In *The Christian Agnostic* he opens with this: "*Not for much longer will the world put up with the lies, the superstitions and the distortions with which the simple message of Jesus has been overlaid. The message of Galilee has been so overlaid with creeds, ceremonies and doctrines, that one can hardly catch the essential message.*"

He goes on to say that any minister, standing in a pulpit, who is not an agnostic is dangerous. Why is he (she) dangerous? Because he pretends to have positive and absolute answers, that he does not have. He lives in the 20th [and 21st] century, parroting back a third century biblical mentality, as though nothing had been learned, thought or discovered in the last 2000 years.

As the religious historian Joseph Campbell put it: "*The majority of ministers either do not understand their material or else are deliberately misrepresenting it, if they know better. They present myth and metaphor as historical literal events. The idea of virgin birth, for example, is presented as historical fact, whereas every mythology (and religious tradition) in the world has included the mythological motif of virgin birth in their legends and folklore. American Indian mythologies abound in virgin births.*"

I commend another book of his to those of you who would like to become more knowledgeable in this area. It is *The Inner Reaches of Outer Space*.

What these scholars are telling us is this: There was a Jesus of history with a simple message. Then there is the 'Christ' mythology created by the early church, using well-known mythological themes of Babylon, Egypt, Persia and Greece. For several hundred years, for instance, early Christians in Alexandria would worship before statues of the Holy Virgin, the Holy Mother Isis. She was suckling her divine child, Horus, whom she had conceived miraculously.

In the 1980s there was in International Symposium held at the University of Michigan in Ann Arbor. Distinguished scholars from major universities in Europe and America presented papers on the Jesus of history and the Jesus of mythology.

Gerald Larue, professor of biblical history, University of Southern California, said this: "*Writers put in Jesus' mouth what the early church wanted him to say. For clergy who know better, why are they not communicating to their parishioners what they know? For clergy who do not know any better, it is simply a matter of ignorance.*"

Van A. Harvey, professor of religion, Stanford University, used these words: "*Anyone teaching Christianity, or the Bible, to college students cannot help but be struck by the enormous gap between what the average layperson thinks is historical truth about Jesus, and what the great majority of biblical scholars know after a century and a half of research.*"

Let it be said that there are ministers keeping their congregations abreast of the latest scholarship in religious studies. The largest Congregational church in America (United Church of Christ), the denomination to which I belong, is the Church of the Beatitudes in Phoenix, Arizona. The Senior Minister there made this observation in a December sermon: "*The key to Renaissance thought is the questioning spirit and the willingness to entertain doubt (agnosticism).*

"*I have no use,*" he said, "*for any religion that does not liberate the human mind to ask great questions. I am impatient with any religion which dampens the inquisitive spirit in humans. I am appalled by any religion that pretends to have firm, final and absolute answers."*

Weatherhead gives us our final reminder: *"Any minister, standing in a pulpit, who is not an agnostic, is dangerous."*

EARTH DAY: A LOVE AFFAIR WITH NATURE

" …we have come to know what it means to be custodians of the future of the Earth – to know that unless we care, unless we check the rapacious exploitations of our Earth and protect it, we are endangering the future of our children and our children's children. We did not know this before, except in little pieces. People knew that they had to take care of their own … but it was not until we saw the picture of the Earth, from the Moon, that we realized how small and how helpless this planet is – something that we must hold in our arms and care for."

> *--Margaret Mead*

Earth Day is fast approaching on April 22. And for some strange cosmic reason, it is always "nature" that fills me with the most poetic love.

I realize that the writers and thinkers, the philosophers and mystics, who have most inspired me have been those who brought me closer to nature and the natural world. Thomas Paine wrote *"men and books lie… only Nature never lies."* And so it is. I have absorbed the thoughts of Annie Dillard… Loren Eiseley… Lauren van der Post… Goethe on "nature"… and Joseph Wood Krutch among many other men and women who have reminded me that I am a part of the natural world and the animal kingdom as Homo sapiens, but so human an animal.

I will never forget how Joseph Wood Krutch came into my life. It was in the basement of the library at Oklahoma State University in Stillwater, Oklahoma. I lived in veteran's student housing on the campus. We were in tornado alley, as they called it then…and still do. It was a night when we were surrounded by tornados. The sirens screamed and everyone went to the basement of the library. I grabbed a new book on the way out of my apartment. It was *"The Voice of the Desert"* by Joseph Wood Krutch. When the "all clear" finally came, I had read the entire book. I knew that I had discovered a most brilliant observer of the natural world and our place in it. How well I remember to this day one chapter on the "Yucca and the Moth." It is nature's most perfect symbiotic relationship. The Yucca and the moth, Pronuba yuccasella, live for each other. Neither could survive without the other. As I am writing these words, I look out of my study doors at the spectacular creamy white blossoms of the Yucca in my yard and I thank the moth who made all of this beauty possible. If you would like to read the insights of this man I would suggest you start with *"The Twelve Seasons."* A sample: *"No government subsidized commission of engineers or physicists can create a worm."*

It is in the early morning hours when my mind/spirit/soul best absorbs the truth and the beauty of these insights into the natural world where truth is to be found. It has always been my favorite time of the day. It is the time of day that can distinguish coarseness from a divine refinement. It is the time of day when a person can look deeply into himself, or herself, and see things and not be fooled. It is the time of day when your vision is clear and the direction of your energies comes into focus. Values and priorities become sharper, issues more clear, right decisions more obvious, and the day begins on a high and noble plane. You are in harmony with yourself and the world.

Erasmus wrote: *"The muses love the early morning, as that is the perfect time for thoughts and study."* Thomas Jefferson wrote that he always arose at first light and walked *"to enjoy the freshness of the new dawn."* Frank Dobie, the brilliant iconoclast of the University of Texas, wrote that, *"he took pre-dawn coffee with Montaigne or Plato and would not wilt the freshest part of the day with the banalities of the news."*

How well I remember the week I spent with Buckminster Fuller. He stood silently every morning at first light, facing east, for about five minutes in meditation. There is beauty… quiet… harmony and tranquility at this magnificent time of the day. The natural world in this little part of the cosmos is preparing to receive the life-giving rays of the morning sun. The juices of life are flowing. It is the time of day when I most clearly remember that we are living in a world of wonder and miracles. How is it that we are all connected in some marvelous and mysterious way to the cosmic dance of life?

The Earth Day celebrations remind me that we live in the midst of, and are supported by, mysteries beyond our comprehension.

In *"Frontiers of Astronomy,"* Fred Hoyle wrote: *"The universe is everything, both living and non-living… both atoms and galaxies. The spiritual and material are ONE. The Universe is a totality of all things."*

Beyond our senses lies a plane of consciousness in which all is related and all is one and all is now. The energy of sun dancing in wood burning fire… a cucumber cucumbering… a flight of geese honking into a north wind… a rising tide crashing and breaking against a resisting beach… a wild stallion with nostrils bugling the pride of the free racing to his mare… mist covering hemlock and pine… a cougar stalking fresh spoor on a mountain trail. It is all one… all natural… all sacred and all divine and all revealed images of the great Mystery that saturates the universe.

My thoughts for Earth Day put my existence in perspective. It is a reality check. All over the world, people are celebrating and honoring their connectedness with each other and the earth. We honor the earth by being aware and doing our part to protect all life on it. We are all family… my little Shih-Tzus are my brothers… my glorious Yucca is my sister… on some profound level.

"The greatest beauty is organic wholeness…
The wholeness of life and things…
The divine beauty of the universe…
Love that… not man apart from that"
                              --Robinson Jeffers

ALBERT EINSTEIN

It is a shame that people think of Albert Einstein only in terms of his genius in physics. He was a prolific and brilliant writer on many subjects.

He was a true mystic who valued intuition and imagination above logic. I quote: *"When I examine myself and my methods of thought, I come to the conclusion that the gift of fantasy, imagination, has meant more to me than my talent for absorbing knowledge."*

"To experience the Mystery is the cradle of true art and true science. He who can no longer wonder, no longer feel amazement, is as good as dead."

"I am truly a 'lone traveler' and have never belonged to my country, my home, my friends or my family. I have never lost a sense of distance and the need for solitude."

Einstein was totally a Bohemian free thinker and free spirit who laughed at the moral prejudices, opinions and judgments of the "masses." He said many times in different ways that he did not look outside of himself to anyone else, or any institution, as an "authority." He said clearly and confidently, *"I am my own authority."*

As the recent subject matter of my Sunday Symposium, it was his penetrating and brilliant views on organized religion that created much interest and confirmation.

Einstein was completely convinced that the vast majority of problems in the world, and especially with individuals, was caused by belief in a "personal" God. An anthropomorphic God who was a "divine window peeker" or a "celestial bellhop" or even a "cosmic hit man."

He wrote: "*Teachers of religion must have the stature and integrity to give up the archaic and superstitious concept of a 'personal' God, a concept that has brought fear and done monumental harm to individuals.*" The idea of a personal God is so very naive.

I am a deeply religious non-believer. This is a new kind of religion. I believe in a "cosmic" religion that has no creeds, doctrines, dogma or churches. What I see in Nature is a magnificent structure that we can comprehend only very imperfectly, and that must fill a thinking person with a sense of humility. I believe only in Mystery.

His Nobel Prize was NOT for the THEORY OF RELATIVITY, as believed by the general public. As brilliant as that was, it was his THEORY OF PHOTOELECTRICITY that won the Nobel Prize.

How does that theory influence your life? The following list of items using that theory will help you. Microwave ovens… TV sets… radios… calculators… auto dashboard indicators. *At the doctors*: fluoroscopy… image intensifiers… X rays. *At the grocery store*: checkout counter laser scanner… fluorescent lights. *On your computer:* screens… printers and indicator lights. The military, of course, practically lives off Einstein's theories.

A few personal notes about this rare and unique individual: He loved his pipes and cigars, and like Carl Jung, had almost a sensuous relationship with his pipes. One time while sailing, his pipe fell in about 3 feet of water and Einstein went down under water again and again to find it. He did. He adored ice cream had all he wanted, free, sent to him monthly by major companies. He hated new clothes and hated socks. He almost never wore socks and wore clothes until holes showed up in them. He was totally "child *like*" (not "childish"), child like in living with daily wonder… surprise… spontaneity… amazement… play… a free expression of emotions. He had few close friends; the only one really was Bohr, another Nobel prize physicist, almost as brilliant as Einstein. He told Bohr one day that: *"your idea is not crazy enough."*

Needless to say, I had to do *two* sessions on this monumental man for my Symposium, and still could not really do him justice.

You might enjoy *The Private Albert Einstein* by Peter A. Bucky, a long time acquaintance who knew him well. What Einstein had to say apart from physics, was truly, equally brilliant

ALBERT EINSTEIN AND THE DALAI LAMA – KINDRED SOULS

Albert Einstein won the Nobel Prize for his THEORY OF PHOTOELECTRICITY, and of course his THEORY OF RELATIVITY is known throughout the world.

His Holiness, the 14th Dalai Lama of Tibet, is the head of state and also the spiritual leader of Tibet.

In every other area of life and living, apart from physics, these two men were truly kindred souls with shared views on almost every subject identical.

The Dalai Lama said, "*I am NOT a Buddhist. I live by the principles found in many of the great spiritual traditions*" and "*We can live without religion and meditation. This is my simple religion. There is no need for temples, no need for complicated philosophy or theology. Our own brain, our own heart is our temple.*"

Albert Einstein said the same thing in these words, "*Teachers of religion must have the stature and integrity to give up the archaic and superstitious concept of a 'personal' God that has brought fear and monumental harm to individual human beings.*" "*I believe in a 'cosmic' religion that has no creeds, dogmas, doctrines or churches.*"

Both men put "compassion" and "love" at the center of their belief system, a guide to the living of their days, a guide that brought happiness into their lives.

"*Man's ethical behavior should be effectively grounded on compassion, nurture and social bonds. What is moral is not divine, but a purely human matter.*" Einstein

"Love and compassion are the true religions to me. But to develop this we DO NOT NEED TO BELIEVE IN ANY RELIGION." The Dalai Lama

"The more you are motivated by love, the more fearless and free your action will be. We can live without religion and meditation, but not without love." The Dalai Lama

With both men, these kindred souls, it was the compassion of their hearts that made them such monumental giants in touching the lives of human beings.

A friend recently reminded me to compare the compassion and love of these two kindred souls, with the life of another creative man, whose motives were suspect. Steve Jobs, of Apple Computers, vowed to his dying breath never to allow cooperation with the Microsoft platform invented by Bill Gates, whose heartfelt compassion formed the Gates Foundation. Even Warren Buffet committed his complete charitable portfolio to the Gates Foundation, a foundation formed from the compassion of a heart.

With both Einstein and the Dalai Lama, emphasis was always on listening to your heart, to look within to your own heart and soul and not to any of all the voices pouring into your head from "outside authorities." *"Your own heart is the only oracle given to you by God."* wrote Thomas Jefferson to his nephew. Einstein wrote, *"I am a lone traveler and have never belonged to any country, or to my friends or family. I am my own authority."*

The Dalai Lama used almost the same words in writing about guides to his own life. *"There is one very important point you must always keep in your mind. No matter what people call you, you are just who you are. KEEP TO THIS TRUTH. How do you want to live? We live and we die. No other person can help us. So consider carefully, what prevents you from living the way you want to live your life."*

It has been a very special path for me lately in reading through volumes of material on these two kindred souls, Einstein and the Dalai Lama, and the true path of life they shared together with ideas so similar it was almost mysterious to me, how in harmony they were. Love and compassion with profound wisdom filled the days of their lives.

Like a pebble dropped in a pond, the ripple goes out far and wide… the wake behind their lives will produce an immortality that will live as long as there are human beings surviving.

WOMEN WITHOUT SUPERSITION

Women Without Superstition: No Gods – No Masters, by Annie Laurie Gaylor, is a very moving, educational and inspirational book. Ninety women are portrayed, women who had virtually no status or respect as individuals. And yet, what a tremendous difference they made in the life of our nation as they challenged the Christian church, the clergy and organized, orthodox religion.

Two women in the book are such inspiring examples of courage, guts, intelligence and integrity.

ELIZABETH CADY STANTON wrote: "*We need the courage to go to the source and strike the blow at the fountain of all tyranny, religious superstition, priestly power and canon law. I can tell you that the happiest period of my life has been since I emerged from the shadows and superstitions of the old theologies.*"

She was the author of the Nineteenth Amendment guaranteeing women's right to vote. She was the first to call for women's suffrage in the United States. She fought tirelessly to free women from legal constraints and from the blight of religious superstition.

Stanton wrote and said over and over again, "*When women understand that religion is a human invention, and that bibles, prayer books, catechisms and encyclical letters are all only emanations from the brain of a man, they will no longer be oppressed by the injunctions that come to them with the divine authority of "thus saith the Lord."*

She said again and again in every way possible that the bible has been used by men for the purpose of keeping women in a state of subjection.

Throughout her life, Elizabeth Cady Stanton suffered abuses and humiliations, and yet she never faltered in her commitment to truth and the emancipation of women, for humanity's sake.

MARGARET SANGER wrote: *"If Christianity turned the clock of general progress back a thousand years, it turned back the clock two thousand years for women. Its greatest outrage upon her was to forbid her to control the function of motherhood under any circumstances, thus limiting her life's work to bringing forth and rearing children. Coincident with this, the churchmen deprived her of her place in and before the courts., in the schools, in art and society."*

In 1914 she wrote, *"The first right of every child is to be wanted. Over-population is the root of the most serious problems in the world."* She was the first to use the phrase "birth control" and she campaigned for *"the right of every woman to total sovereignty over her own person."*

No safe method of birth control was known in America in 1912. Women were not only trapped into economic and social slavery, they were also in biological slavery.

The church hated Sanger and the medical profession denounced her. She was often jailed and once flew to England to avoid a potential forty-five year prison sentence.

When the wrath of governmental and clerical opinion fell heavily upon her, Gandhi, who in his own country realized the blight of overpopulation, came to her defense. So did Clarence Darrow and H.G. Wells.

One of the greatest tributes paid her or any historical figure came from the pen of H.G. Wells who wrote, *"Alexander the Great changed a few boundaries and killed a few men. Both he and Napoleon were forced into fame by circumstances outside of themselves and by currents of the time, but*

Margaret Sanger made currents and circumstances. When the history of our civilization is written, it will be a biological history and Margaret Sanger will be its heroine."

As we revere those whose lives stood for truth against popular custom, political power and clerical arrogance and ignorance, we must remember all of those women who stood boldly by their convictions with their written and spoken words.

The power of the written word! The immortality of the written word. Great ideas are a force for change. There is an immortality in that, as the great Roman and Greek thinkers 3,000 years ago still remind us. "*The spoken word perishes: the written word remains.*" (Vox audit perit: litera scripta manet.)

It is through their written words that Stanton and Sanger, Emerson, Jung, Jefferson and Madison, still today inspire, motivate, encourage, teach, awaken, stimulate us still, even more so than in their own time.

The women without superstition…no Gods…no masters are still giants of today in our own time, and we stand on their shoulders and carry their courage and their truth onward.

A FESTIVAL OF POETS

Truth is to be found in all of the arts: in music, from Bob Dylan to Duke Ellington to John Lennon; in theatre and film, from *Death of a Salesman* to *Clockwork Orange* to *Judgment at Nuremberg* to *Edward Scissorhands*; in literature and poetry, from the great classics of Plato and Hemingway to Toni Morrison and George Orwell; in art, from Rembrandt to Picasso to Andy Warhol; in dance, from Isadora Duncan to Martha Graham to Michael Jackson.

For this week's column, I am going to be celebrating the "language of life"…the music of language that is poetry, through the works of some of the poets that have moved me, and inspired me, and been my heroes. There is more truth to be found in poetry than in all the philosophy ever written, said Octavio Paz, Nobel prize winner in literature and poetry, who was called "the soul of Mexico."

Anne Kingsford, writing about "the poet," used these words: "*The great continual cadence of universal life moves and becomes articulate in human language. The daughters of earth love thee, the water-nymphs tell thee their secrets, thou knowest the spirit of all silent things. Thou art multiplied in the conscience of all living creatures and the pulses of the infinite deep…vibrate in thine own.*" This short paragraph is only a beautiful sample of the entire lengthy essay.

One of my giant heroes of literature and poetry, from Nebraska, is JOHN NEIHARDT. He was Poet Laureate of Nebraska, Poet Laureate of Missouri, Chancellor of the American Academy of Poets; his bust is in the Rotunda of the State Capitol in Lincoln, Nebraska.

He is the author of *Black Elk Speaks*, a book called, by Carl Jung, "*one of the spiritual classics of our life time.*"

He could write, in poetry, *The Cycle of the West*, of the profound history of the plains Indians, the Lakota and Cheyenne. He would write some of the most erotic and beautiful love poetry in existence in *A Bundle of Myrrh* in 1907.

Here is an excerpt from *"The Twilight of the Sioux,"* The Village of Crazy Horse.

"Meanwhile among the Powder River breaks…
Where cottonwoods and plums and stunted oaks
Made smug his village of a hundred smokes.
Crazy Horse was waiting for the spring…
When the moon was icy and the blue snow whined…
or when for days the world went blizzard blind.
Something holy moved about the town…
Crazy Horse."

A Bundle of Myrrh, Neihardt's beautiful love poetry, was read by a young woman in Paris, who was studying sculpture with Rodin at the time. Her name was Mona, and they began a correspondence. She prayed, *"Dear God…don't let him be married."* She sailed the ocean, crossed the country by train, and arrived at the Omaha depot, where young Neihardt was waiting for her with a marriage license. They had never met until that moment. They were joyfully married until her death, fifty years later. Their ashes were scattered together over the Missouri river, following his death.

From *A Bundle of Myrrh*: "The Witless Musician"

"She is my violin!
As the violinist lays his ear to his instrument
That he may catch the low vibrations of the deeper strings,
So I lay my ear to her breast.
I hear her blood singing and I am shaken with ecstasy;
For am I not the musician?

She is my harp – I play upon her.
I touch her, and she trembles as a harp with the first chord of
a revery.
I lay my hands upon her with that divine thrill in my finger-tips,
That reverent nervousness of the fingers,
Which a harpist feels when he reaches for a ravishing chord,
Elusive chord from among the labyrinthine strings.
I am a musician for the first time!
I have found an instrument to play upon!
She is my violin – she is my harp!"

In 1956, the National Poetry Center awarded Neihardt the Medal of Honor as foremost poet in the nation.

His range of writing has been monumental, from a pre-eminent authority on the plains Indians, the Lakota and Cheyenne, from *Black Elk Speaks* to the glorious erotic love poetry of *A Bundle of Myrrh*.

When he was interviewed on Dick Cavett's show, Neihardt, at age 93, recited *The Village of Crazy Horse* from memory. It lasted about 10 minutes. Cavett said he had never received so much mail applauding a show in his entire career. Neihardt came to hold the belief that a dynamic spiritual pattern is at work in the cosmos, and that our destiny is spelled out in such a pattern. I think you can now understand why he is one of my heroes…a brilliant poet who turned language into music; he gave us the language of life.

THE LANGUAGE OF LIFE

During the month of May, continuing into June, at my Sunday Symposium at the Palm Springs Tennis Club, we are celebrating "The Language of Life" and the life and works of the poets who have given us this language.

I started on the first Sunday with JOHN NEIHARDT, whose bust is in the rotunda of the state capitol in Lincoln, Nebraska. He was the Poet Laureate of Nebraska, as well as Missouri, the author of the classic *Black Elk Speaks*, the author of many books of poetry including *An Epic of the West,* and some of the most beautiful love poetry ever written in *A Bundle of Myrrh.*

The next Sunday I presented STANLEY KUNITZ, twice Poet Laureate of the United States, who spoke "the language of life" in a profound use of language. Next, I used the work of BILLY COLLINS, as he also was twice Poet Laureate of the United States. The troubadour, BOB DYLAN was also a part of the poetry of that Sunday.

I think of all the topics I have presented at my Sunday Symposium, this is my favorite subject for the same reason that Bill Moyers put into words: "*Poets live the lives all of us live, with one big difference. They have the power to make the experience of life both magical and real. The life they reveal is our own.*"

Poetry is language in its most exalted, delighted and concentrated form. Maya Angelou has said, "*Poetry is music written for the human voice.*" Poetry readings are concerts of sheer joyous sound. The "soul of Mexico," Octavio Paz, put it this way: "*when you say life is marvelous, you are saying a banality. But to make life a marvel, that is the role of poetry.*" When you listen to poetry being read well, you are a witness to the marvel, you are experiencing the marvel.

The New York Times recently had something to say about this subject. *"Poetry readings have moved out of smoky cafes to become a staple of the cultural scene."* Poetry readings are held at over 150 places in the New York area alone. The renaissance of public poetry is over the entire nation. The Elliott Bay Book Company in Seattle schedules 70 readings a year, and the poets of our day are putting powerful energy and new idioms into our language.

Against the vulgar images of advertising that daily infect us, against the barbaric rhetoric of politics, poetry stands as a beacon to human feelings and senses, as well as the human imagination.

Stanley Kunitz wrote, *"Poetry is the most solitary, and most life-enhancing thing that one can do. It is a struggle because words get tired. We use them and abuse them. A word is a utilitarian tool, and we have to re-create it to make it magical."* Poems are carriers of memories. Naomi Nye explained poetry by using beautiful words: *"Poems allow us to savor a single image, a single phrase. Just think how many people have savored a haiku poem over hundreds of years. It slows you down to read a poem. You read it more than one time. You read it more slowly than you would speak to someone in a store. And we need that slow experience with words."*

There are no limits to what poetry can do, and how words can move people to heights beyond their wildest dreams.

As a former Marine Corps pilot, the words of *High Flight* are the language of life for many of us who lived daily in the air. The poetic words of John Magee can move me still to moist eyes:

"Oh! I have slipped the surly bonds of Earth
And danced the skies on laughter-silvered wings;
Sunward I've climbed, and joined the tumbling mirth
of sun-split clouds, — and done a hundred things

You have not dreamed of — wheeled and soared and swung
High in the sunlit silence. Hov'ring there,
I've chased the shouting wind along, and flung
My eager craft through footless halls of air…
Up, up the long, delirious, burning blue
I've topped the wind-swept heights with easy grace.
Where never lark, or even eagle flew —
And, while with silent lifting mind I have trod
The high untrespassed sanctity of space,
- Put out my hand, and touched the face of God."

John Magee, a 19 year old RCAF fighter pilot, wrote the moving and eloquent words of *High Flight*, just before his plane crashed.

"To make life a marvel, that is the role of poetry." Magee made flying a marvel.

Octavio Paz said: "When you say life is marvelous, you are saying a banality. But to MAKE life a marvel, that is the role of poetry."

And so it IS. My Symposium is enjoying this series on "The Language of Life."

COURAGE AND CONTROVERSY

I have received letters by the hundreds over the past 30 years saying, "I want to congratulate you on your courage, writing as you do. How I admire your courage" and so forth.

Now my question: "Why should it be considered "courageous" to write the materials in my columns that can be found in any history book in any library in this country?"

Why is it "courageous" for me to write material that is accepted, and taught in the departments of religion in every major university in this country, or the world for that matter?

For instance, I write: "Our Founding Fathers, Jefferson, Madison, Adams, Franklin. Washington, Paine, were all Deists, classical humanists, who did not believe that Jesus was divine, and they did not believe that the bible was anything other than "literature," and they did believe that the Christian church was a giant tyranny." People write me and say "what courage to write like that."

Well, what I have written can be found in the writings of the founding fathers themselves. It is hardly "courageous" to write facts and truth that are obvious and available in historical records.

Or, I write, "The virgin birth stories about Jesus are mythology, and virgin birth has been a universal theme in all religious traditions." What courage, people write me. Well, again, it is hardly "courageous" to write what is accepted and taught in religion and literature classes in major universities all over the world.

Now, please think through the word "controversial." I have lost count of the times I have been introduced as "that controversial religion columnist."

Again, how can any statement or subject be "controversial" if it is taught and accepted in major universities all over the world?

All "controversial" really means is that you have never heard about it. You have never heard your minister talk about these things, or he/she would be out of a job, and it is unlikely you have ever read about any of these issues in magazines or journals.

If you have believed that two and two are five, and some scholar comes along and tells you that two and two are really four, then they become "controversial." It is no wonder that we are a nation of religious illiterates, as I have written in previous columns.

The media, THE NEWSPAPERS, MAGAZINES, INTERNET AND TELEVISION, along with popular politicians, FEED THE ILLITERACY by placating, publishing, and courting Bible belt superstitions.

When newspapers, magazines, etc. publish religious articles that are an embarrassment to any religiously educated person, they are choosing an active role in sustaining superstitions and religious ignorance.

The fact that there are illiterate readers of a newspaper who still believe that the center of the cosmos and everything on the earth was "created" only 4000 years ago is no excuse for any newspaper to publish articles that support such ignorance and give support to such religious darkness and blindness.

It is neither "courageous" nor "controversial" to write about material that can easily be found in scholarly books in any library in this nation. For those who still like the label "controversial," I can only offer an observation by Benjamin Rush, signer of the Declaration of Independence:

"Controversy is only dreaded by the advocates of error."

TIME AND ARMAGEDDON

From now until 2012, we are going to be buried and suffocated, staggering in the onslaught of superstition and ignorance. It is all going to be masquerading under the phony and scary heading of "prophecy." This virus of illiteracy can even affect the Oval Office, as with President Reagan's weird speculations about an imminent arrival of Armageddon in the Middle East. We are going to be smothered in the months ahead by radio, books, television and movies out to make a buck on the gullibility of the American public. It will be open season on reason, rationality and religious literacy.

What seems to be missing from the brain/mind (I use the words loosely) of most of the hysterical is the fact that TIME IS FICTION. TIME is man made. A history of man-made calendars would enlighten many. On many calendars, the millennium would already have come and gone and you did not even know you missed it.

Christian fundamentalists, of course, are panting for the day, but with the vast majority of the world it is a non-event.

In the JEWISH calendar, the year 2000, for instance, was 5760 and no big deal. For MUSLIMS, who date their calendar from the prophet Muhammad's move from Mecca to Medina, the year 2000 would be the Islamic year 1420. Muhammad said that the "day of doom" would not come for another 50,000 years. So relax, folks. You will not even be around to see it happen.

The ISLAMIC calendar follows the cycles of the moon rather than the sun and their year of 2000 is 1418 In the CHINESE Lunar calendar it is now the year 4695, over 315 years away from the next millennium. HINDUS are now in the midst of a calendrical cycle that has over 350,000 years ago until it ends. You won't be around for that either. So you can plainly see that for the vast majority of the world, our millennium was a non-event if ever there was one.

With our American Indian concepts of time, this entire subject is absurd. Most American Indian languages do not have past and future tenses. They reflect rather a perennial reality of the NOW. Their accounts of creation, for example, do not tell of a PAST time but rather of processes that are eternally happening. The Maya and Hopi "prophecy" have to do with the evolutionary expansion of human consciousness. "Hopi time," writes Benjamin Lee Whorf in *Language, Thought and Reality,* is true psychological time. If we inspect "consciousness" we will find no past, present or future… everything in consciousness IS and is together now.
What an interesting contrast in mentalities. Christian fundamentalists, with other "Prophecy" addicts, waiting for the world to go up in flames, with volcanoes and earthquakes going off like a holiday fireworks celebration, and California sliding into the ocean, to the beautiful thought of the American Indian looking for a new stage in the expansion of human consciousness.

Let's see now… let me think… how many hundreds of times has the end of the world been set for a date on our calendric system? Oh my, I have lost count. And imagine, look. I am still here, as are you. And the "Prophecy" addicts have gone back to their Ouija board.

THE SEXUALITY OF JESUS

This is a continuation of my series on biblical superstitions that do significant damage to the lives of those who believe them to be true.

The judgmental moralists, thin lipped, quoting the bible, are always hard at work. Witch hunting in bedrooms. Poor things. They can hardly get out of bed in the morning without knees knocking… hands shaking… lips quivering. The sexual world that they have to face each day is filled with fantasized goblins… devils… evil spirits and bogeymen. Church history would hardly support their bigotry and bedroom witch hunts.

The Sexuality of Christ in Renaissance Art received rave reviews from all quarters. It was written by Leo Steinberg who originally delivered the material at a Lionel Trilling Seminar at Columbia University and was honored by the College Art Association of America with its annual award. Some will find it offensive… those who find all expressions of sexuality offensive.

The sexuality of Jesus is very obvious in the paintings. Jesus was a Hebrew male, a man in the fullest sense and a sexual human being in the same sense that all men are sexual human beings. And yet for some neurotic and weird reason, many want to keep this subject behind drawn shades or else locked in the closet. Many times in study groups and seminars, I have presented material that would indicate Jesus was either married or had a mistress; and after time to think it over and absorb the material, there's a gradual relaxing with the subject from those in attendance.

Even Martin Luther faced this issue squarely, saying in his book *TableTalk* that Jesus no doubt had sexual relations with Mary Magdalene as well as "other women." That Luther was a gutsy guy. He also wrote, "*If your wife is cold, call the maid.*"

Luther was not alone in his robust attitude toward sexuality. Pope Julius II, by a papal decree, established a "sacred" brothel in Rome that flourished under his successors, Leo X and Clement VII. The earnings of the brothel supported the Holy Sisters of the Order of St. Mary Magdalene. (Church history is not as dull as you might think.)

But, back to the sexuality of Jesus.

Ancient Judaism valued married life highly. They disdained celibacy. There are NO instances of life-long celibacy in the entire Old Testament... or the Apocrypha... the Qumran scrolls, the Mishnah or the Talmud.

Our 20th century sexual liberalism in many places is not the issue here. What is the issue are the sexual attitudes of first-century Judaism; and it is recorded that Jesus traveled around the countryside in intimate companionship with a group of women, including Mary Magdalene.

His entourage included, "women who ministered unto him of their substance." (Luke 8, 1-3) His women followers remained faithful to him right through to the end, as compared with Judas and Peter, for instance. And our New Testament Gospels say that only Mary Magdalene and her women attended the tomb of Jesus.

The duty of becoming betrothed shortly after puberty was axiomatic in ancient Judaism. Marriage was a religious duty taken seriously, and the Gospel of Mary, discovered in Egypt, leaves no doubt about the matter, suggesting that Jesus and Mary Magdalene were married.

In the Gnostic Gospel of Philip, we read, "*there were three who walked with Jesus at all times. Mary, her sister Salome and Magdalene, who is called his partner.*" In another sentence, Mary Magdalene is called the "spouse" of Jesus and tells how he "kisses her often."

73

The treasure of the Gnostic gospels, discovered only as recently as less than 50 years ago, have many references to the sexuality of Jesus. Professor Helmut Koester of Harvard University writes that the collection of sayings in these Gospels include traditions much older than the Gospels of the New Testament, and also much closer to the actual life of Jesus.

In the Gospel of Philip are these words, "The companion of Jesus is Mary Magdalene. Jesus loved her more than all the disciples and used to kiss her often on the mouth. Jesus said to the other disciples, *"Why do I not love you as much as I love her?"*

This is NOT such a new theme, really. D.H. Lawrence and Nikos Kazantskis made the issue of the sexuality of Jesus central to two of their works. And of course one of the most haunting and beautiful songs to come out of "Jesus Christ, Superstar" was the tender rendition of "I Don't Know How to Love Him" sung by Mary Magdalene to Jesus.

The Sexuality of Christ in Renaissance Art introduces readers to a very legitimate dimension of Jesus, the man who was fully human. Many will find it refreshing and far more in touch with reality than the Jesus of mythology that the Christian church has presented for year after dogmatic year…as history rather than the fiction it is.

LEVITICUS AND HOMOPHOBICS

This series is on biblical superstitions and the damage they have done to the lives of the people who believe them.

Don't you just love the homophobics, the bigots, and clowns of the Christian Coalition and the fundamentalists? "*The bible is God's word,*" they yell at us… "*the bible is true… every word… and by God himself… and we live by that book… we live by it… and what it says… we do. And it says right there in Leviticus 18:22 that you shall not lie with a male as with a woman; it is an abomination.*"

Now, if we live by that archaic, ignorant and superstitious book, just look who else is going to hell. Ah, what fun. Practically all the political leaders in Washington, that's who. "*And God said you shall not marry a woman divorced from her husband*" (21:7). How I love that bible. There went Reagan… Dole…Gingrich…Buchanan and all those other big shot Republicans and Democrats who have broken God's law and married divorced women.

And the fun and games have just started. Look at Leviticus 20:10. I love that bible. "*If a man commits adultery, both the adulterer and adulteress shall be put to death.*" There goes almost everyone in Washington, D.C. and the Pentagon and Sacramento all burning in hell. What a show. That bible is right on as to who is going to burn… and it is darn near everyone you see by the time you finish God's list. The gays are going to have a lot… a very lot… of company while they are all burning together.

You ranchers and farmers have had it…like I mean HAD IT. Leviticus 19:19 orders you that… "*you shall not let your cattle breed with a different kind.*" How I love that God. He tells those ranchers and farmers, "*Now Claude…I've seen you cross-breeding Charolais and Angus. And those white face*

Herefords you crossed with Longhorns. How could you have missed my orders?"

And what's next in God's orders to keep the gays company? My oh my… all the clothing shops… fabric shops… clothing designers all headed straight for hell. Oh my… tears flood my eyes.

Leviticus 19:19 orders us as follows: *"You shall never wear a garment of cloth made of two kinds of material."* But, hey God, I like to wear shirts and jackets of linen and wool… linen and cotton… polyester and cotton and so on… and oh my, all those nice people burning in hell for breaking God's laws. How much more can we take? What, you mean we have barely started on who is going to burn? What a sense of humor he has… that God. I say "he" for no Goddess would issue such a list of stupid, crank commands.

You farmers have had it man. Read this: *"You shall not sow your field with two different kinds of seed"* (Lev. 19:18). There goes that mixed seed for hybrid corn. And those beautiful fields of alfalfa and clover are going to burn… burn like in hell.

You remember Nancy Reagan who used to live by astrologers. Wonder what her horoscope said the day she started burning… with new perfume on yet. Leviticus 19:31: *"do not turn to mediums or seek them out, to be defiled by them."* Oh Nancy you looked so pretty, before you started burning.

And hey… one thing God said, that really gets your attention. WOW… you talk about child cruelty. Here is a great one for your smart ass kids (Leviticus 20): if they give you any lip, why… simple… kill 'em. Forget all that weak stuff like grounding them or cutting their allowance. Simple solution God said: Just kill 'em. That God was the original Judge Roy Bean of West Texas: "we will give 'em a fair trial and kill 'em."

So I say to all the Christian Coalition phonies and fundamentalists: "If you say Leviticus is God's word on gays and lesbians, then the ENTIRE BOOK OF LEVITICUS is God's word and are God's laws… so LIVE IT… walk the talk… or GET OFF IT."

EMBRACE THE MYSTERY

When all the words have been written, and all the phrases have been spoken, the great mystery of life will still remain. We may map the terrains of our lives, measure the farthest reaches of the universe, but no amount of searching will ever reveal for certain whether we are all children of chance or part of a great design.

And who among us would have it otherwise? Who would wish to take the mystery out of the experience of looking into a newborn infant's eyes? Who would not feel in violation of something great if we had knowledge of what has departed when we stare into the face of one who has died? These are the events that made us human, that define the distance between the stars and us.

Still, this life is not easy. Much of its mystery is darkness. Tragedies occur, injustices exist. Bad things befall good people and sufferings are visited upon the innocent. To live we must take the lives of other species, to survive we must leave some of our brothers and sisters by the side of the road. We are prisoners of time, victims of biology, hostages of our own capacity to dream.

At times it all seems too much, impossible to accept.

We must stand against this. The world is a great mysterious place, and its possibilities are infinite, governed only by what our hearts can conceive. If we incline our hearts towards the darkness, we will see darkness. If we incline them toward the light, we will see the light.

Those of great heart have always known this. They have understood that, as honorable as it is to see the wrong and try to correct it, a life well lived must somehow celebrate the promise that life provides. The darkness at the limits of our knowledge; the darkness that sometimes seem to surround us is merely a way to make us reach beyond certainty, to make our lives a witness to hope, a testimony to possibility, an urge toward the best and the most honorable impulses that our hearts can conceive.

It is not hard. There is in each of us, no matter how humble, a capacity for love. Even if our lives have not taken the course we had envisioned, even if we are less than the shape of our dreams, we are part of the human family. Somewhere, in the most inconsequential corners of our lives, is the opportunity for love.

If I am blind, I can run my hand across the back of a shell and celebrate beauty. If I have no legs, I can sit in quiet wonder before the restless murmurs of the sea. If I am wounded in spirit, I can reach out my hand to those who are hurting. If I am lonely, I can go among those who are desperate for love. There is no tragedy or injustice so great, no life so small and inconsequential, that we cannot bear witness to the light in the quiet acts and hidden moments of our days.

And who can say which of these acts and moments will make a difference? The universe is vast and is a magical membrane of meaning, stretching across time and space, and it is not given to us to know her secrets and her ways. Perhaps we were placed here to meet the challenge of a single moment; perhaps the touch we give will cause the touch that will change the world.

KRISHNAMURTI: THE SAGE OF OJAI

Ojai, California, is nestled in the radiant mountains just south of Santa Barbara. I say "radiant" because famous there is what they call their "pink moment" when every evening at sunset, all the mountains and valley are covered with a rich and bright "pink" color that is gorgeous to witness.

Ojai has a reputation of being one of the artistic and cultural centers of the United States. Many of the creative giants of the world beat a path to the "Sage of Ojai" KRISHNAMURTI a mystical genius who pointed their lives in a new generation: Joseph Campbell...Joan Halifax...Julian Huxley Thomas Huxley...D.H. Lawrence... John Lennon... David Bohm (Nobel in physics) ...Jonas Salk...Charlie Chaplin.....and too many to name.

In my 18 years of my SUNDAY SYMPOSIUM I have for some strange reason not spent an entire session on this "Sage of Ojai" though often quoting him. On October 21, the first date of the new Fall Edelen Book Corner (and Symposium)....I am going to cover the life and contribution as well as the genius of this "sage" KRISHNAMURTI.

Based on my own life experiences, at 90 years old, I soon realized that everything I was reading in his writings was true and accurate and could change individuals and society by evolving into a more enlightened consciousness. Such as the following paragraphs:

"*I maintain that truth is a pathless land, and you cannot approach it by any path whatsoever, by any religion, by any sect. That is my point of view, and I adhere to that absolutely and unconditionally. TRUTH, being limitless, unconditioned, unapproachable by any path whatsoever CANNOT BE ORGANIZED, nor should any organization be formed to lead or coerce people along a particular path. I concern myself with only one essential thing TO SET MAN FREE, I DESIRE TO*

FREE HIM FROM ALL CAGES AND ALL FEARS, and not to found religions, new sects, nor to establish new theories and new philosophies."

Oh my, when I first read that, bells and lights were going off in my head. So profound, so eloquent, so clear, so TRUE.

And again: "*All authority of any kind, especially in the field of thought and understanding, is the most destructive and evil thing. Leaders destroy the followers. You have to be your own teacher and own disciple. You have to question everything that man has accepted as valuable and necessary.*"

Many giant thinkers have made observations about our pathetic educational system. Robert Hutchins....Buckminster Fuller who said every normal child is born a genius until parents and teachers de-geniuize them as fast as they can....Bertrand Russell...and on … but few have written about it more clearly than our "Sage of Ojai."

"*Conventional education makes independent thinking almost impossible. Conformity leads to mediocrity. We are turning out, as if through a mold, a type of human being whose chief interest is to find security, to become important... to have a good time with as little thought as possible.*

Conventional education puts an end to spontaneity and breeds fear. (Einstein wrote brilliantly on that subject.) Fear of life kills the human spirit. Our entire upbringing and education have made us afraid to be different from our neighbor... afraid to think contrary to the established pattern of society, falsely respectful of authority and tradition."

"*Intelligent revolt comes through self knowledge.. through the awareness of one's own thought and feeling....this highly awakened intelligence is INTUITION..... the only true guide in life.*"

In the 1970's, Krishnamurti met often with then Indian Prime Minister Indira Gandhi, with whom he had far ranging and very serious discussions.

This "Sage of Ojai" spent the majority of his life there where the valley and mountains have their daily "pink moment." He crossed over to "the other side" in that spot at 91 years of age in February 1986. The wake that this life left behind him will fan out and expand as long as there are human beings on this earth.

.

STARTING A NEW DAY

In an issue of *Palm Springs Life* magazine, I had a short essay on the theme of becoming aware of the joys of each moment, as they come to us, one by one.

But so much depends on the way we start each new day. I might say even that everything that follows during any given day will be directly related to the first few hours of that day. Whether the day unfolds on a high and noble plane, or turns out to be only a survival contest to be endured.

I have a friend who refuses to turn on the television or radio, or even read a newspaper until later in the afternoon. It is a valuable insight. It can make a remarkable difference in how the day progresses.

Many years ago I started reading biographies and autobiographies of great and noble men and women whose own lives were centered and balanced, and who had made contributions far beyond the normal. I was intrigued by the fact that practically all of them started each new day in similar fashion, in a calm, tranquil, quiet and meditative manner. Yes, even if you have to arise early ahead of the children.

It has been my routine for over 50 years to start the day before first light, between 4 and 4:30 a.m. the most glorious time of the day, especially in the spring, summer and early fall.

Thomas Jefferson wrote that he always arose at first light and walked to enjoy *"the freshness of the new dawn."*

Erasmus wrote, *"The muses love the early morning, as that is the perfect time for thought and study."*

J. Frank Dobie, the brilliant iconoclast of the University of Texas, wrote that he took his pre-dawn coffee with Montaigne or Plato and *"would not wilt the freshest part of the day with the banalities of the news"* but would *"rather start with the rhythms of the natural day."*

Carl Jung writes of his living with some of the primal peoples of Africa and describes the manner in which they started each new day: *"Sunrise was the most sacred hour of the day. The people would raise their arms to the sun, breaking over the horizon. The gesture means, 'I offer the Universe my living soul.' I too joined them, drinking in this dawn glory, with insatiable delight, in a timeless ecstasy."*

How well I remember the week that I spent with Buckminster Fuller. He stood silently, every morning in first light, facing east for about five minutes in meditation.

There is beauty, quiet, harmony, vision and tranquility at this magnificent time of the day. The natural world in this little part of the cosmos is preparing to receive the life-giving rays of the morning sun. The juices of life are flowing. Roosters are announcing their presence. You will never see any painting more spiritual than dawn breaking. No church hymn will ever lift your heart higher than the early morning chorus of the birds.

It is the time of day that can distinguish coarseness from a divine refinement. It is the time of day when a person can look deeply into himself, or herself, and see things and not be fooled. It is the time of day when your vision is clear and the direction of your energies comes into focus. Values and priorities become sharper, issues more clear, right decisions more obvious and the day begins on a high and noble plane. You are in harmony with yourself and the world.

A healing thought might be to re-examine the way you use the first few hours of each new day. The first hour of the morning is the rudder of the day. And Erasmus reminds us:
"THE DAWN IS ALWAYS A FRIEND TO THE MUSES..."

THE COSMIC DANCE

People often ask me "what are you?... what do you believe? Buddhist, Taoist, Christian... what?" In a joking mood I may tell them that I am a Druid, Taoist, Agnostic, Shaman.

But, when serious, I tell them I live within the historical stream of mysticism... and that world view, cosmology, or philosophy of life, is the same whether one lives in a Taoist society, Buddhist, Christian, or secular. With this consciousness, the ultimate reality (or God) is apprehended directly without any mediation. Subject and object become One in a timeless, spaceless act that is ineffable and gloriously joyful. Beauty and light and love are seen pervading the entire universe, including the individual self, now merged in Oneness with all creation. It is a "cosmic dance".

The experience transcends the reach of any language. The Mystery is within us and every leaf, every atom, every molecule... with all. The universe is a totality and an interrelatedness of all things. For the cohesive Mystery within that totality, we use the word symbol "God". It is creative love in a "cosmic dance."

Many still want to apply the word symbol "God" to something "out there," separate and distinct from us "down here" on this planet earth. It is always God and something else: God and us, God and creation, God and the creatures... as if the word "God" were a symbol for some "It" out there.

Dualism constantly separates man and woman from God, nature from man, and spirit from matter. We must rid ourselves of the dualism that infects so much of our orthodox religious views of the earth and universe.

Several years ago a Zen Master was lecturing at Stanford University. He opened his address by stepping up to the front of the stage, leaning toward the audience and saying: *"Man against God. God against man. Man against nature. Nature against man. Nature against God. God against nature. A very, very funny religion."* A roaring ovation followed his remarks.

Today's physics and quantum mechanics confirm that the classifications of animate and inanimate are archaic and invalid. Of course, Eastern religions and the American Indian traditions have been saying that for centuries.

In *The Dancing Wu Li Masters,* the author Gary Zukav writes that "contemporary physicists are expressing (are defining) themselves in the language of the mystics. The distinction between the "in here" and the "out there" no longer exists. Dr. Donald Andrews of Johns Hopkins University used these words: *"Every time you lift your finger, the farthest galaxy feels the impulse."* Or, as Physicist James Jeans wrote: *"Modern physics has reduced the whole universe to waves, and nothing but waves."*

All galaxies, stars, planets and human beings are manifestations of waves. I am talking about the Oneness, the interrelatedness of everything that is tied Together, by the Mystery, that is known only through experience. The "Cosmic Dance"… *"will you, won't you, will you, won't you, will you join the Dance,"* asked Alice in that memorable story.

The cemeteries of history are filled with the graves of the dead gods and goddesses "out there": Astarte, Baal, Demeter, Ishtar, Horus, Isis, Osiris, Jupiter, Thor and all the others. Man's quest to understand his relationship to the cosmos created them all, presented by priests and clergy who dominated through fear.

Not until man began to identify himself as One with all of creation did he begin to understand the mystical experience and to find God within himself. We are alive Now, awake Now, and only in the Now do we experience the beauty and joy of the Mystery within the "Cosmic Dance".

The mystic Henry David Thoreau gives us the last word: "*If for a moment we make way with our petty and trivial selves and cease to be but as a crystal, which reflects a ray, what shall we not reflect! What a universe will appear radiant around us…*"

PHYSICS AND MYSTICS

"I believe in mystery and that also we experience some of the most beautiful things in life in a very primitive form. In relation to these mysteries I consider myself to be a spiritual man. He who cannot stand in wonder and awe before the Mystery is as good as dead." --Albert Einstein

What few realize is that the most brilliant of our Nobel Prize winning physicists were also mystics. Their writings on this subject are the most beautiful I have ever read. Mysticism and Physics are fraternal twins.

Students of both believe in a mystical world view that embodies the world as spiritual and material; classifications of organic and inorganic, animate and inanimate are archaic and invalid.

One of the most treasured books in my library is *Quantum Questions* edited by Ken Wilber, "the mystical writings of the world's greatest physicists".

In Sir Arthur Eddington's *Defense of Mysticism* he writes: "*A defense of the mystic would run something like this. We have acknowledged that entities of physics can from their nature form only a partial aspect of reality. How are we to deal with the other part? It cannot be said that the other part concerns us less than the physical entities. Feelings, purpose and values make up our consciousness as much as sense impressions. We mystics are the music makers, and we are the dreamer of dreams wandering by the lone sea breakers and sitting by the desolate streams, world foresakers, on whom the pale moon gleams; yet we are the movers and shakers of the world forever, it seems.*"

Max Planck, Nobel Physicist, writes in *The Mystery of our Being*, "*The mystical element in human nature must be recognized and cultivated if all the powers of the human soul* *are to act together in perfect balance and harmony. The greatest thinkers, of all ages, have been **deeply mystical souls**. Science cannot solve the ultimate mystery of nature and we are therefore part of the mystery that we are trying to solve. Music and art also attempt to solve, or express, the mystery."*

Winner of the Nobel Prize in Physics, Louise de Broglie in his *The Mechanism Demands a Mysticism* states: *"The increased body of machines awaits a supplement of soul and the mechanism demands a mysticism. Humanity groans half crushed under the weight of the "advances" it has made. Man has need of a mystical supplement of the soul, and he must force himself to acquire it promptly before it is too late."*

From *The Mystic Vision* Erwin Schroedinger, Nobel in Physics, writes: *"To say 'I am god' sounds blasphemous to the orthodox Christian. But the insight of this truth is not new. The earliest records date back some 2500 years or more, from the early great Upanishads. The recognition that the personal self equals the omnipresent, all comprehending, eternal self was in Indian thought considered to represent the quintessence of deepest insight into happenings of the world. The strivings of all the scholars of the Vedanta was to assimilate in their minds the grandest of all thoughts. All mystics, of many centuries, independently, yet in perfect harmony with each other, have described the unique experience in his or her own life."*

My own is as follows: Several years ago I made my fourth and last backpacking trip to the bottom of the Grand Canyon of Arizona. I went **alone**. It was the scene of one of the most moving spiritual experiences of my life.

I was sitting on the sand beside the Colorado River. A slight breeze rustled cottonwood leaves, like an aeolian harp. Evening light faded into darkness and was soon replaced by a full moon, hovering, so near and immediate that I put out my hand and touched its face… the source of all that is… the energy, the Mystery… that, for want of a better name, we use the word symbol "god", yet knowing that only silence has the true name. There was only time and the river singing and flowing. I could not possibly sleep. I was experiencing the origin. Rocks close by were over three billion years old. I was the only human, and I was **One** with the river, the cottonwoods, rocks, full moon and breeze.

There is no way I can share the depth of that experience with words. And here we are at the heart of Zen and Taoism. They say, rightly, that "experience transcends the reach of any language," and truth is always found through experience, and never from any outside authority. A new awareness reached my consciousness, not from any known source, book or speaker, but through channels unknown… an experience that led to the recognition within me of the **oneness** of all that is in time or space. I had experienced more of that mystery we call Life..a brief interlude between two greater mysteries that are yet **One**.

As I identify more deeply with a mystical view of life, I find myself opened to a constant awareness that "in here" and "out there" no longer exist. My unity, my oneness with all creation is clear and becomes evident in my everyday experiences, and the "Mystery" unfolds through every significant event.

The celebrated Zen Master Suzuki once was asked what was the point of mysticism. He said that before he understood he saw mountains as mountains and water are water. When he made some progress he no longer saw mountains as mountains and water as water. But after more progress he again saw mountains as mountains and water as water. The student asked, well, what was the difference between the first and last time, when he saw mountains as mountains and water as water. Suzuki said "well no difference at all, except the second time you are walking about two feet off the ground."

DESERT LOVE SONG

I am writing this love song under a full August moon. Since I am a Cancer, a moon and water child of the universe, I have often wondered as I wander, what cosmic astrological energy force is there that is within me during these periods. Some spirit within me has moved me to write of this desert love. Why do I feel that need to write about this? It is almost as if I had no say in the matter, as if some form of universal energy made the decision.

I am not alone in that observation. Many writers, musicians, poets, artists, scientists, thinkers have come to that conclusion. I have found it fascinating, in a synchronistic way, that three psychics over the last 50 years, in different parts of the country, have told me that I would spend the last 30 years of my life in the desert, where I was meant to be, working with a group of free thinkers, free spirits, on a spiritual quest. And so it has happened in just that way. Three psychics, far removed from one another in difference parts of the United States.

The month is August. I have my calendar of the soul that is far more accurate than the printed one on my desk. It is in August that we have just passed through the wonder and miracle of the summer solstice, recently celebrated. The dazzling shimmering light of this period balances the winter solstice. It is the Yin-Yang of the universe, the cosmic dance of complementary opposites. The heat waves radiate out from the mountain rocks that jealously guard our home. The animals find shade and the flowers wait patiently for their daily drink. I live surrounded by miracles and I realize that we humans are only a very small part, a unit of one, symbiotically related and dependent upon all of the other billions of protoplasmic relatives.

How is it that we are all connected in some marvelous and mysterious way to the cosmic dance of solstice and equinox?

This "something unknown doing we know not what." I am in awe gazing at the flower outside my study window. A long time ago, there were no flowers, and then just before the Age of Reptiles there was a soundless explosion that lasted over a million years. It was the emergence of the angiosperms, the flowering plants. And from flowers came the mystifying emergence of man. My flower seeds have a long memory and I too, as I remember that my very existence as Homo sapiens depends on these flowers.

And I think that the flowers of a rainy spring, and the grasses of a showery summer are good and beautiful and sufficient, even though they will shortly vanish.

Under this August full moon, having followed the summer solstice, I am reminded again, that we must come to terms with non-physical reality. We came from non-physical reality and we will return to non-physical reality, two realities which are yet ONE. We are being influenced every moment of our lives by other energies from non-physical realities. It is like ultraviolet light, microwave light and infrared light and many other ranges of frequencies that coexist with our visible light spectrum and yet are invisible to us. How many other non-physical energy frequencies coexist with us and are yet invisible? The solstice and equinox reminds me that we live in the midst of and are supported by mysteries beyond our comprehension. "*This Mystery*" wrote Albert Einstein "*that is the source of all true art and true science.*"

Writing my "love song" I remember an austere desert spoke of by God to the Hebrews. The desert spoke of the stars to the Arabs and astronomy came into being. Mystics and philosophers, artists and poets with those questing for insight and truth, have always gone to the desert for inspiration.

The desert to me speaks of silence and solitude, endurance and flexibility, visions and peace, tranquility and balance. The living forms of the four-legged and the two-legged, the winged ones of the air, and the crawling ones on the ground adjust to the heat of the day and the cold of the night. And the great lush oasis of the desert canyons reminds me of the Yin and Yang of nature and how it cares for its own.

Long after our artificial cities have crumbled, the desert, with its timeless beauty, will call once again to those who have survived.

When confused and fragmented by city chaos, it is in the desert that in silence… and solitude… we find our spiritual oasis, a spiritual vision that inspires a "love song."

A SPIRITUAL UNION – MOUNTAIN AND DESERT

In the Coachella Valley, where I live, there exists what could be one of the most powerful energy fields on the planet, with Mt. San Jacinto at near 11,000 feet hovering over, protecting, watching, loving the desert of the eternal valley called Coachella, the result of an ancient lake that covered the entire valley and long ago receded to the ocean.

The sun, like a jealous lover, hovers over the desert in a protective manner, unique and unknown to rain forests and the endless waters of the ocean.

The desert reduces everything to essentials, to the basics of whitened bone. The desert, perhaps more than any other place on earth, speaks of silence, simplicity and solitude. The desert calls to men and women who being wasted away by the stress, confusion and anxieties of city life, yearn for a spiritual retreat, an escape from the demon time, the clock and the calendar that that so enslave us.

All great spiritual traditions began, from a desert or a mountain, with the vision quest of one lone, single individual who, in solitude and silence, saw through the veil of the superficial into those realms and dimensions of reality that were of the timeless and eternal.

As their vision spread, it often descended lower and lower, like rivers rushing downhill, by those who understood it not, or used it for corrupt ends. Born in a lonely place of solitude and silence, in an exalted and inspired state of mind, the vision of Jesus, Buddha, or Lao Tzu became polluted as it entered cities where masses of human beings prostituted the vision for their own ends and vested interests.

Many sensitive people today, aware of the corruption of the spiritual vision, retire to the desert or the mountain top overlooking the desert, to seek in silence the vision, to again return their lives to the source, to the Mystery that has been so corrupted by the masses. The desert, eternally, has called to such individuals.

It is no accident that monotheism was born in the desert. A mosque is a stylized Oasis. The Bedouins found the desert visions of one God their own experience of the austere and the sublime. In the desert, a concept of one God has no competition as is found in rain forests and lands of lush vegetation where many gods compete for loyalty and allegiance. Likewise, it is recorded that Jesus retired to the desert for solitude and meditation.

Everything in the universe is composed of complimentary opposites. Yin and Yang, as the Buddhist and Taoist traditions remind us. We see this so beautifully illustrated in the symbol of the Tai Chi disc. When you are doing Tai Chi, you are moving to the rhythms of complimentary opposites. A desert sunrise as seen from Mt. Sinai, or that same sunrise as seen from Mt. San Jacinto in the first blush of dawn light reminds me that we live in the dazzling, daily reality of the truth and beauty of complimentary opposites, the Tai Chi disc of Yin and Yang.

It is the mountain and the desert, wedded in cosmic harmony, that create the powerful spiritual energy I experience in the Coachella Valley.

Mountains are sacred. All native people have known that, as well as many more sophisticated cultures. And when you combine, in a complimentary relationship, a sacred mountain with an eternal desert, there is a spiritual force, a dynamic energy and a cosmic power present that influences everything in its radius.

D.H. Lawrence described it in these words: "*In the oldest religions, everything was alive, not supernaturally, but naturally alive. There were only deeper and deeper streams of life, vibrations of life more and more vast. So rocks were alive. A mountain had a deeper, vaster life than a single rock. A person needed to bring his spirit or his energy into contact with the life of a mountain.*"

Rocks and mountains have been sacred in almost every spiritual tradition. Mt. Sinai and the Temple of Mount Jerusalem, the "black stone" in the Kaaba shrine at Mecca, for the Lakota, the Sioux in the plains, it was Mt. Harney in the Black Hills. "*Inyan the rocks are holy*" said Lame Deer. The chants of the Pebble Society of the Omaha tribe praised "*the mountains and the rocks.*" The Rock of Ishi in Japan is perhaps the purest example in any religion of the spiritual presence of a rock. The Rock of Ishi represents creative divinity. The rock reminds us that we, as humans, are a part of the universe and one with universal divinity. Rocks are the central focus of meditation in Zen gardens. Mount Kailus is considered the throne of the god Shiva, and has been called "the spiritual heart of the world." It is the center of the universe for Hindus and Buddhists and forms the hub of China and India. Mt. Rainier was called "Tachoma" or "the mountain that was God" by the Indians of our Northwest. The Taos Pueblo of New Mexico is bounded by four sacred mountains and the San Francisco peaks are sacred to the Hopi as well as the Navajo. For our own desert people known as the Cahuilla, there were the Santa Rosa Mountains, as well as Mt. San Jacinto.

Our sense of the sacred is awakened when we use the mountain as the focus of our meditations. The rise of a peak in the morning mist. The glint of moonlight on an icy ridge. The gold of sunlight on a distant summit can awaken the fact we live in a world of glorious beauty and mystery, absorbed with all of our senses awakened. We respond with awe and wonder and a sound of joy pours forth from our throat that we cannot hold back. "Ah," we say, and it is in that "Ah" that the depth of our spirit comes forth and we are awake as we sanctify the moment and the place where we are.

THE LANGUAGE OF THE SOUL

MUSIC is the language of the soul and the cathedral of the human spirit. More human beings have been moved, healed, inspired, up-lifted, redeemed and transformed by music than by all of the philosophies and contradictory theologies ever written. If a "God" is beyond human comprehension, then "theology" is a pseudo-science without a subject matter and the theologian is one who does not know what he is talking about. But, through music, joy, love, sorrow, tears, lamentation, laughter and meditations find a voice that fills our hearts.

Dr. Lewis Thomas, former Dean of the Yale University School of Medicine, writes these words in *Thoughts on Listening to Mahler's Ninth Symphony*: "*Music is the most profound mystery of human existence. No one has the ghost of an idea about what music is, or why we make it and cannot be human without it. How does the human mind make music on its own, before it is written down and played? Nobody can explain it. It is the greatest mystery of the human mind.*"

Can you see now why I call it "the language of the soul" and the "cathedral of the human spirit?"

The range of music that has touched my spirit over the years brings pure joy from my bank of memories, of standing in evening parade at the Marine Corps Barracks in Washington, D.C. where the Commandant lives, and listening to the concert band with tears running down my cheeks. Music and the spirit. I walk into my study at home to relax and I turn on the tape of Barry Manilow's *Singin' With the Big Bands* and my study is filled with "I Can't Get Started" and I feel happy, memories of that magic time of warm days and soft nights. When I want to soar into the sacred realms of the divine I listen to that breathtaking goddess, Jessye Norman singing

Gounod's "Sanctus." Or the vision of Bach soaring through the organ pipes of St. John the Divine.

Or if I want the absolute beauty of notes combined to celebrate not only human eros and amor, but being surrounded by the miracles of the natural world, I fill my study with the gorgeous sounds of Antonia Carlos Jobim, with his "Meditations" written for eros and amor… *"Yes, I love you so… and that for me is all I need to know… I wait for you meditating… on how sweet life will be when you are back to me."*

That soul and spirit-filling music moves my "meditations" past amor to the glory of nature and the words written so eloquently by Joseph Campbell:

"We are the children of this beautiful planet that we have lately seen photographed from the moon. We were not delivered into it by some god, but have come forth from it. And the Earth, together with the sun, this light around which it flies like a moth, came forth from a nebula, and that nebula, in turn, from space. So that we are the mind, ultimately of space, each in his own way, at one with all, and with no horizons."

My "meditations" include the miracle of amor and eros, as one with the miracle of the sacred earth, from whence we came.

Music… where did this mystery come from? Where but from months in the womb, listening to the heart beat of the mother. We enter this world with the cosmic rhythm of our mother's heart that sings music into our souls, and we cannot be human without it.

Music is the only universal tongue… the language of the human soul… the Cathedral of the Human Spirit.

TO LIVE WITH WONDER

If we are fortunate, at some point before we die, we can discover WONDER. For we who have become so preoccupied with gaining and spending, with winning and losing, have lost sight of the miracles around us. Wonder is the capacity of sustained joy and awe. Wonder is a sense of freshness and spontaneity. Every day is a surprise party. Life is a cafeteria of delights, a new flower, a hummingbird hovering, a cucumber cucumbering.

To sense the ultimate in the common and in the rush of the passing, stillness in the eternal is to live with wonder, with "Ah."

The purpose of religion for thousands of years has been to put human life into direct contact with the life of the cosmos, mountain life, desert life, cloud life, sun life, moon life, water life, rain life, snow life, plant life, animal life, storm life, rock life, and so receive energy, joy, and transformation. That is why the seasons of Solstice and Equinox are so important in the celebrations of so many traditions.

Today, physicists are telling us that their understanding of "reality," the nature and activity of the universe is bringing us closer and closer to the perspective of the ancient Eastern religions, especially Hinduism and classical Taoism.

We are a part of the cosmic dance, and all is one. Physicists assure us now that rocks and flowers dance with the dance of life. Trees dance to the wind. Salmon and trout and porpoise dance and leap with a ballet of grace and rhythm. Planets dance to beautifully intricate laws, even as do atoms. There is no line between the sacred and the profane, the supernatural and natural, the divine and the human. ALL is natural, ALL is sacred. ALL is divine. It is asked of us even as the carpenter asked in *Alice in Wonderland*: *"Will you, won't you, will you, won't you, will you join the dance?"* A recently translated Dead

Sea Scroll records a disciple asking Jesus, *"Master, how can we get into the Kingdom of Heaven?"* Jesus answers, *"Follow the birds, the beasts, the fish, and they will lead you in."*

Classical Taoism has been saying that for 3000 and more years. The Old Master of Taoism, Lao Tzu, born about 600 B.C. was immaculately conceived by a shooting star, according to legend. He did not preach or organize any doctrine or theology. He spoke only of our at-oneness with the universe and the harmony that exists between all things. The Tao (pronounced "Dow") does not refer to a supernatural "god" out there, somewhere.

Do you want to see the Living Tao? Look into a wood burning fire and see the sun's energy dancing, as captured by photosynthesis. Watch a bird in flight, soaring on the current and never stopping to analyze or explain the wind. Listen to the sound of rain, which needs no translation. Watch a salmon leap up the next set of rapids. Watch a bee gathering pollen. The Tao is the way of ultimate reality. It says, *"Get yourself in tune and harmony with the natural rhythms of nature and the universe, and then let yourself flow without strain, tension and anxiety."* It is a perspective and view of life that can be used daily in the busiest office in downtown San Francisco or New York City. It changes the way you approach problems.

In our busy, rushed, calendar-filled world of appointments and meetings and conferences, it can save us from migraine headaches, high blood pressure and stress problems. Whether you are a Christian, Jew or Agnostic, the beautiful themes of Taoism can still become a part of your days and activities. It can enrich your view of the world and enlarge your understanding of reality.

The flow of life is like the flow of water. If you are thrashing and flailing around, you tire and exhaust yourself and drown. If you relax and float and flow with the tide, it carries you gently. So it is with life. It is as was said by a nomadic teacher named

Jesus: "*Consider the lilies of the field, how they grow. They neither toil nor spin. Consider the birds of the air. They neither sow nor reap. Why be anxious?*"

Living in the flow helps you to re-discover WONDER. The wonder of being alive in a world surrounded by miracles.

Here's a lovely story of Taoism that illustrates the question of, "why be anxious?" A Taoist was walking along a road with a heavy bucket, filled with fresh honey, carried on a pole over his shoulder. The bucket slipped off the pole and fell to the ground, breaking, with honey all mixed into the dirt. A man on the side of the road rushed over to the Taoist who just kept walking, and yelled, "*Hey, your honey bucket fell and is all over the road back there.*" The Taoist just kept walking and said, "*I know, I heard it fall.*" It was broken. What could he do? Gotten in a stew… raised his blood pressure… yelled… cursed… worried… but NO, he just kept walking, saying, "*I know. I heard it fall.*" It was over. Ahead was life, and joy, and wonder.

Living in the flow, flexible, helps to rediscover wonder. The rigid pine breaks. The willow bends in the strong wind and returns to its original shape.

A life lived in the flow of nature's rhythms, calm, helps us to experience the beauty of the dance, of life… events… relationships. It is mandatory for living a life filled with the wonder of our days and existence. It is living with WONDER.

KRISHNAMURTI: A MANTIS EXPERIENCE...

I recently spent two wonderful days at Ojai, California soaking up the spiritual center of the Krishnamurti home, library, and grounds, including the "pink moment" of the Ojai valley at sunset. For those of you who are regular readers of my columns or *Symposium* newsletters known as "E Blasts From Bill," you are well aware of the details of that remarkable visit. And you may remember what I described as a moment of mystery and magic. When I stepped out of my quarters to return home, there waiting for me was a Praying Mantis. I have seen very few in my lifetime. My mind immediately went to all that I knew, and had read about this "manifestation of God come to Earth" in the thought and belief system of the African Bushman: A divine messenger.

When I returned home I went to my book shelves and pulled out *A Mantis Carol* by Sir Laurens van der Post. On the cover of this beautiful book are these words: "If you read no other book this month, this year, this decade, read this one." -The Christian Science Monitor (a paper many times voted one of the most outstanding newspapers in the U.S.)

"Mantis" is the Greek word for "prophet" or "seer," a being with spiritual or mystical powers. The praying Mantis shows the way. In the Arabic and Turkish cultures a mantis points pilgrims to Mecca, the holiest site in the Islamic world. In Africa it helps find lost sheep and goats. In France, it's believed that if you are lost the Mantis points the way home. "Follow Mantis" means putting that core aspect of yourself, your foundation of Spirit, at the helm and let it direct your intellect and ultimately your life.

"Meet the eye of a mantis and feel the presence of God. God looking at me through the eye of the Mantis." The Mantis points the way and the path to relieving the "great hunger" in

103

our lives. "The name of this great hunger was the hunger for love and for a way of life lived in love out of love for the love of it alone." "This love, this calling for wholeness in life. The gratitude to life which comes flooding in over one as one experiences again how pervasive and always near is the mystery of love as though it were in the blood and bone of ourselves." The Mantis became a symbol of meditation and contemplation.

In China the mantis has long been honored for her mindful movements. She comes when we need peace and calm in our lives. A list of praying mantis symbolism would include: Stillness, Creativity, Patience, Calm, Balance, Intuition.

As we left the Krishnamurti spiritual center I thought how very mystical and magical it was to look into the eyes of a mantis and be told to recover a center for balance, to go within and meditate, to lead a life of calmness and wholeness… all being a part of the central message of Krishnamurti who said again and again he wanted to free people from their cages of conformity, moderation, fear… finding their security through groups and group identification… and lead them to a path of confidence and joy, living as the unique individuals they were meant to be. "Following Mantis means putting your unique spirit at the helm and letting it direct your intellect and your life." It is a timeless message for us that is in perfect harmony with the message of Krishnamurti. I had not seen a Mantis in years and years. And the fact that one was there waiting for me, as I departed the spiritual center of this rare and unique man, was for me magic and mystery that truly transcends language.

DOGS OF VALOR: DOGS OF EMINENCE

In my 50 years of writing newspaper columns and essays, no other column has been such a "labor of love" as this one on the WAR DOGS of combat who brought many members of our fighting military home safely.

My journey for this emotional and educational experience started with my personal friendship with world-renowned sculptor, A Thomas Schomberg and his wife Cynthia, who often attend my Sunday Symposium in Palm Springs. Thomas was the artist who created the WAR DOG MEMORIAL at March Air Force Base in Riverside, California, at the entrance to the Air Museum. It was built by the support of veterans and the public, without one cent of government money, in an effort to honor each and every valiant War Dog and their efforts to save lives and prevent countless casualties.

In Tom's own words: "*It is to illustrate the sacrifice that these two figures have made under combat circumstances, and to illustrate the bond between humans and their canine friends.*"

A veterinarian serving in Vietnam wrote: "*without these dogs there would be a lot more than 50,000 names on the Vietnam wall.*"

Dogs in warfare have a long history starting in ancient times. "War dogs" have been trained for combat and to be used as scouts, sentries and trackers. War dogs were used by Egyptians, Greeks, Persians, Samarians, Slavs, Britons and Romans. Frederick the Great used dogs during the "seven years war" with Russia. And of course ALL American wars to the present day of Iraq and Afghanistan. In Vietnam captured Vietcong told of the fear and respect that they had for the dogs. The Vietcong even placed a bounty on lives of handlers and dogs. It has been estimated by the Pentagon that war dogs saved over 10,000 U.S. lives in Vietnam alone.

Memorials to these magnificent dogs can be found from Ft. Benning, Georgia to the Marine Corps primary base in Quantico, Virginia.

As I write this column my memory goes into rewind... remembering the magical psychic relationship I have experienced with the dogs who have shared my 90 years of life. You can understand why my eyes were moist as I spent a day recently at this outstanding War Dog Memorial at March Air Force Base, and inside the Museum, the moving and beautiful displays as tributes to these brave and loyal dogs. As a Marine Corps pilot for 12 years, when I came to the tribute of the Marines at Camp Pendleton, my moist eyes added an extra light tear.

Tragically, the War Dogs of Vietnam were never allowed to come home... in fact, were euthanized... because there was no way for them to return. It was the year 2000 that President Bill Clinton signed a law that finally allowed dogs of war to come home and to be adopted. It was the same year the War Dog Memorial was dedicated. Cynthia Schomberg wrote me of that magical day in 2000:

"Immediately after the large black cloth was removed from the WAR DOG MEMORIAL, a row of 50 to 75 "service military dogs" with their trainers walked in a single column from the back of the audience around the side to the front where the statue stood.

The lead dog was carrying an empty chain dog collar in his mouth and dropped the collar at the foot of the statue. Upon a single loud command from the head trainer, all the dogs sat and began to bark at once.

Shortly after that there was a fly over by Air Force fighter planes. Then taps was played. There was not a dry eye in the entire area. I still get the chills thinking about it.

Shortly after that a long line of hundreds of Veterans from WWII, Korea and up, lined up and were given a single stem rose, then promptly filed up to the statue where some touched the bronze dog and placed the rose on the statue.

The thing that was most amazing to me were all the stories from the Veterans, some told for the first time in 30 years. Families told both Tom and I that their father/husband would never talk about their experiences until now. The moving experience of that day at the WAR DOG MEMORIAL unveiling helped many of those vets to open up."

It was a day to be cherished forever by those in attendance. As I looked one last time before starting home, my thoughts were these: what a magnificent symbol of the comradeship, protection, sacrifice and love between man and dog.

It was a magical and moving moment. For me, it was an experience never to be forgotten. When I arrived home I sat down and looked into the eyes of my four legged soul mate who lives here with me. We love each other unconditionally. It is a bond that every man or woman with their dog, understands. It is no cliché to say that it is a bond that truly....transcends language.

A MARINE CORPS JEWEL

The "jewel" or "treasure" of which I write is the United States Marine Corps Air Station at El Toro, California. On Saturday, Sept 22, I was interviewed here in my home for four hours by the oral history department of the State University of California, Fullerton. The interview was about my time stationed at El Toro and flying there, flying both the F4U Corsair and the F7F Tiger Cat. The purpose of the University project is to preserve the rich history of Marine Corps Aviation and the El Toro Air Station, as well as the contribution to Orange County and the United States.

The day before my interview I traveled west to El Toro. To call it a "sentimental journey" would be a monumental understatement. To stand on that runway where I had taken off and landed hundreds of times filled my heart with memories... the excitement of Marine Corps Aviation, the bonding of pilots, and the glorious history of flying "where never lark or eagle flew".

My mind was filled with the precious memories of driving out to that base every morning through orange groves and flowers, giant glorious trees, lining the roadway. Driving from our housing area at the "lighter than air" base nearby, and then commuting from our new housing area at Oceanside, Camp Pendleton, until buying my first home at Anaheim, California. Those were the days before Disneyland.

I was asked at the interview many questions about my impressions and feelings of being stationed there. I loved it. My first answer was that the beauty of the place overwhelmed me. El Toro was truly a jewel and treasure that should be preserved forever. It was a magical time there for me, a young Marine pilot, spreading my wings daily to fly with the best of military pilots. It was a time of growth and maturity for me in my many years as a Marine Corps pilot. I lived with life and death daily. The Corsair killed many young pilots due to the dangerous design of the plane. The 'gull wing' the extra powerful engine with torque that would flip you over on your back if full throttle was added without immediate compensation by the right rudder to offset the pull. El Toro made a most significant contribution to my own growth and skills as a Marine Corps pilot. Skills that led me on in that career to becoming one of the six personal pilots to the Commandant of the Marine Corps, General Lemuel Shepherd.

Today, the "higher ups" of Orange County want to make a park around the air station for the general public. They call it "The Orange County Great Park." It will need to be designed with great sensitivity, not to dilute the treasure that was, and is, the beating heart… the El Toro Marine Corps Station. They call it the "Marine Air Station, EL Toro and Mid-Century Orange County."

The interview with me was finally over after *four* hours, but we all agreed that we could have continued for another four hours easily and still not covered all of my impressions and feelings about that unique place — that jewel — and what it contributed to the lives of the Marine pilots who spread their wings, and flew out of that magical piece of earth, called Marine Corps Air Station, El Toro.

CHRISTMAS AS POETRY

There was always one worship service, above all others, that I loved doing in my church. It was the Christmas Eve candlelight service at 8:00 and 11:00 p.m. with standing room only. In my Congregational church I made it a celebration of the human spirit, with song and dance, poetry and literature, meditation and joy.

I will never forget the spectacular ballet dancer performing Tai Chi to Gounod's "Sanctus" as sung by Jessye Norman. The dancer said that the first time she practiced it she just stopped and cried; it was that moving for her.

We always closed with all lights out and everyone holding candles and singing "Silent Night, Holy Night" led by guitarists playing in the balcony, like the original Tyrolean alpine folk melody. The organ would then come in with such glorious chords we all had a near "out of body" experience. Some skeptics would always say to me "*I can't sing that stuff. I don't believe any of that.*" And I would tell them, and the congregation, "I don't believe it either as factual or historical theological statements. That's not what it is all about. You miss the point if you do not experience the beauty of the myth, a solstice myth that goes back by thousands of years before Jesus was ever born."

Our bloodstream runs into the veins of the gods, Greeks and Romans, Egyptian and Persians and barbarians in the Germanic forest. For thousands of years before Jesus, Greeks and Romans sang their hymns in honor of their gods and goddesses at the winter solstice and celebrated with gifts and singing, drinking and decorations, with flowers, palms, mistletoe and holly.

I would suggest that the congregation see life as a poem and the solstice season as poetry, and suggest that they picture themselves as participating in the poetry through the celebration of ritual. That is the purpose of mythology and what it is all about. THEY GOT IT. They understood it and loved it as a celebration of families and love, sharing and joy, meditation and mystery, with a consciousness of the sacred in life and the holy dimensions of existence.

George Santayana, one of the most brilliant teachers at Harvard University, and one of the great poets and philosophers of our time, was an agnostic. Yet every Christmas Eve, he and his wife attended the midnight candlelight mass. His friends teased him: *"George, you know you do not believe any of that Jesus stuff. Why do you go?"* *"Ah"* replied Santayana *"but it feeds my spirit."* He got it. He was not interested in the absurdities and stupidity of archaic doctrines and creeds. He was a poet, and he and his wife were participating in the poetry of life through a solstice ritual that could be over 25,000 years old.

D. H. Lawrence made the observation that there are two kinds of truth: a truth of facts and a truth of truth. A truth of facts has to do with names, dates, places and so forth. But a truth of truth is revealed to us through mythology, legend and folklore.

The truth of truth has to do with the inner world of the imagination and emotions. They reveal the inner shape and contour of our minds, our longings, needs and our spirits and soul where we live and dream and hope and imagine and create. There is an inner world where we create our own truth. We take the myths, folklore and legends of an ancient time and rewrite them according to our own needs, hopes and fears for our own time.

Truths of Truth will not qualify as facts. There are those who want us to live without myth and poetry and feelings and emotion. They want us to live only by the truth of facts. What they would substitute is technology, science and ideologies as a means of discovering meaning and celebrating values. To live only by truths of facts can impoverish and stunt our lives and as Carl Jung reminded us is *"a disease of our time."* A virus of the mind.

For instance, many times have I stood on the banks of Jenny Lake in the Grand Tetons of Wyoming in both the pre-dawn and sunset hours. I have gazed across that placid, clear lake to the opposite shore where the Grand Teton rises, soaring almost vertically to over 10,000 feet and guarded on each side by the other slightly lesser peaks. Tumbling down into Jenny Lake, gently brushing the base of the Teton and making a joyful noise is the water whose origin was the snow above Lake Solitude, high in the high country where I have often hiked.

Now, an analyst is quite correct in saying that this lake, the water, is nothing more than two parts of hydrogen to one part of oxygen. That is an important truth of facts. And this hydrogen and oxygen combined is merely obeying the law of gravity as it pushes igneous rocks out of the way, or goes around them. That is true and factual. An analyst is quite correct in saying that these Tetons are granite consisting chiefly of crystalline quartz, mica and feldspar. Those are truths of facts and very important. But, to stop there is to impoverish my life.

Something else, another truth is also there and is truth that is more than analysis. That "something" else is of my heart, emotions, mind, spirit and soul. It has to do with reflections, receptivity, appreciation, insight, responsiveness and sensitivity to beauty and feeling, to a truth of truth that has often left me breathless and with moist eyes.

And so I know that December the 25th has nothing factual or historical to do with Jesus, even as I know that Jenny Lake is only hydrogen and oxygen. I know that "virgin birth" and "stars" and "shepherds" and all the other biblical Christmas stories were common mythological themes, or motifs, that can be found in all the other religious traditions of that part of the world. Other virgin births celebrated during the solstice period included: Marduk, Osiris, Horus, Isis, Mithra, Saturn, Sol, Apollo, Serapis and Huitzilopochi. I know those are truths of facts.

But, the truth of truth that speaks to my heart is the joy of celebrations with the love of family and friends, and bringing back to our memory the truth that we are all children of the same Source and the same Mystery. Life, so called, is only a brief interlude between two great Mysteries which are yet One. This season reminds me of spiritual insights that are a truth of truth and that touch the depths of my being, my existence, more profoundly than any truth of facts.

This Solstice season is poetry, and you are a part of the poem. May the poetry of life fill your hours and days. That is my wish for you.

THE FUTURE REQUIRES COURAGE

We live in an exciting and stimulating period of history. One age is dying... and the new age is not quite born.

We see radical changes in sexual patterns, lifestyles, marriage styles, women's roles, family structures, education, energy, religion, the Christian church and in almost every conceivable aspect of life. We can withdraw in anxiety, or we can become negative and pessimistic. If we choose either of these paths, we forfeit our chance to participate in the creation of the future.

To live in this age, or any age, requires an enormous amount of courage, faith and willingness to take risks. But to participate in the forming of a future is to create. And courage, risk-taking, creativity and faith are the attributes that have continually reformed the structure of civilization.

What is creative courage? It is the willingness to pursue new forms, new symbols and new patterns of truth. The alternative is stagnation.

Every profession — technology, diplomacy, business, arts, medicine, law — requires those who possess a creative courage. Certainly that is true in teaching and the ministry.

At the end of *A Portrait of the Artist as a Young Man*, James Joyce has his young hero write these words in his diary: *"Welcome O Life... I go to encounter for the millionth time the reality of experience and to forge in the smithy of my soul the uncreated conscience of my race."*

In other words, every creative encounter is a new event, and every time requires another assertion of courage and faith and involves risk. I especially like the words, *"to forge... the uncreated conscience of my race."* Joyce is saying here that conscience is not something handed down ready-made from

Mount Sinai, nor the Sermon on the Mount, given once and for all.

Why is creativity so difficult? Why does it require such courage? Why is it such a risk-taking venture? For the very reason that it does contribute to the process of creating a new conscience for the race. It is not just simply a matter of clearing out debris from an ancient age, of clearing away dead norms, defunct symbols and myths that have become lifeless. It is not that simple.

The major risk is that creativity provokes the jealousy of the institutional gods. That is why genuine, authentic creativity always takes such courage.

An active battle with the gods occurs, whether the gods be an institution, a church, a government, or those protecting an outmoded image of a supernatural God. Courageous creativity always provokes the jealousy of, and outrages, the gods. In ancient Greek civilization Prometheus challenged Zeus, and Zeus was outraged. The same truth was presented in the myth of Adam and Eve. "God" is outraged at the audacious courage of Adam and Eve.

The relating of rebellion and creative courage to religion is hard for many people to swallow. In religion it has not been, by and large, the flatterers of the popular God who have been ultimately praised. It has been the insurgents and the rebels who are praised by history and immortalized, among them Socrates, Jesus and Joan of Arc.

The pharaoh of the 18th dynasty of Egypt, Akhnation, challenged the entire corrupt priesthood of Egypt saying, *"you are enslaving people with your superstitions… your ignorant beliefs."* Zoroaster was persecuted; Buddha made scathing attacks upon Hindu corruption in his time; Luther and Schweitzer were excommunicated from their church.

The biblical prophet Micah had the courage to speak: *"There is no anthropomorphic god up there waiting for your sacrifices and rites and rituals. No. All that is required of you is to do justly and love mercy and to walk humbly."*

In one of Renan's philosophical dramas there is a dialogue in heaven where Gabriel speaking of the Earth and its skeptics says to God... *"If I had thine omnipotence, I would quickly reduce those wicked atheists to silence."* But God, benevolently replies: *"Ah Gabriel, thou art so faithful, but thy faithfulness has made thee so narrow. Learn my special tenderness for those who deny me. For what they deny is the image, grotesque and abominable which has been put in my place. In all the world of idolaters, they alone, the doubters and deniers, are the only ones who really respect me."*

The cemeteries of history are filled with the graves of the dead gods... Astarte, Baal, Isis, Horus, Osiris, Jupiter, Thor. It is time to bury at least one other god, the god of vengeance and anger, a theological policeman whose beat is the universe, a heavenly trigger man, a celestial hit man who has a contract out on some earthly humans.

There is a far greater archaeology than digging for lost cities. It is an archaeology of the mind, aimed at uncovering the foundations of the authentic city of the soul, covered with all the debris of conventional and antiquated religious systems. We must dig through, layer by layer, until once again each of us can experience in our own lives the fresh new spirit that speaks again "let there be light... and there was light..."

ABOUT THE AUTHOR

William Edelen was born in West Texas and spent his boyhood there and in Oklahoma City. He flew for twelve years as a U. S. Marine Corp, pilot, flying both fighter planes and transports in World War II and Korea. This included one tour of duty as one of six personal pilots assigned to the staff of the Commandant of the Marine Corps, Washington D. C.

He requested a discharge and returned to Oklahoma State University where he received the Bachelor of Science degree in Horticulture and Biology. He then entered McCormick Theological Seminary (on the campus of the University of Chicago) where he received his Masters degree in Theology.

Edelen's history

- Two years graduate studies in anthropology, University of Colorado.
- Lecturer of religion and anthropology, University of Puget Sound, Tacoma, Washington
- Weekly columnist for many western newspapers
- Special studies with Joseph Campbell, whom the New York Times called "The pre-eminent scholar in Comparative Religions and Mythology."
- Active ordained Presbyterian and Congregational minister, 30 years

117

- Author of *Toward the Mystery, Spirit, Spirit Dance, and Earthrise* (chosen by the National Methodist Women's organization as one of their national study books in 1986.)

In 1990 he received a grant from the Annenberg Foundation to promote religious literacy through writing and speaking. He started a Sunday Symposium at Oakmont in Santa Rosa, California, a weekly meeting where he lectured for 45 minutes, followed by 30 minutes of discussion.

In 1994, after moving to Palm Springs, California, he started a similar Sunday Symposium at the Palm Springs Tennis Club. It is an outstanding group of free thinkers that meets every other Sunday except August and September. His home base is Palm Springs where he now lives.

He has lectured widely in the Western states from Colorado, Idaho and New Mexico to California. He has written a regular weekly column for many Western newspapers including The Desert Sun of Palm Springs, The Chieftain of Pueblo, Colorado, The Idaho Statesman of Boise Idaho and The News Press of Santa Barbara, California.

His website is: www.williamedelen.org. This site publishes all of his weekly columns plus other information. The Edelen Ministries is an IRS approved charity that exists for the purpose of educating and raising the level of religious literacy.

"William Edelen is an original thinker in the oldest of thinking worlds, that is, thinking about God. He's in love with the truth. Edelen dares to do his own thinking. He has wide experience to enrich that thinking."
  --Buckminster Fuller

"Your wonderful piece of writing which was waiting for me when I returned is the best reward I have received to date from this year's activities."
  --Joseph Campbell

"With your keen intellectual awareness and your background in the biological science, you are obviously an unusual asset. I do want to tell you that I have come to have an increasing sense of gratitude to men such as you who uphold the spiritual values, without which the life of man is nothing. I salute you."
  --Loren Eiseley

"Bill, I could not have been more pleased than when I was listening to your lecture. This is the sort of scholarship that I am always interested in."
  --Charles Schulz, "Peanuts" creator

"Your overall record of citizenship is indeed distinguished and for which I salute you. May I express admiration for the character of your career."
  --Walter Annenberg

"Your lectures are indeed superlative…
You must keep writing…
Keep speaking…
You are much needed…"
  --William O. Douglas, U.S. Supreme Court Justice

"The Sage of Palm Springs."
  --Palm Springs Life Magazine

10015738R00074

Made in the USA
San Bernardino, CA
03 April 2014